Embracing

Projects for Grown-ups to Keep and Treasure

Child Art

Barbara A. McGuire

Published by

Krause Publications
700 East State St., Iola, WI 54990-0001
Telephone 715-445-2214
www.krause.com

Please call or write for our free catalog of publications. To place an order or obtain a free catalog, please call 800-258-0929. Please use our regular business telephone 715-445-2214.

Library of Congress Catalog Number 2001090427
ISBN 0-87341-985-5

Cover photo credit: Chloirali, age 11, Cyprus. ICAF.

Acknowledgments

When you define art, you usually decipher whether it is visual art or performing art. Although this book is presented on behalf of visual art of the children, there is definitely a group of performers: parents, educators, friends, corporations and communities that have given of time, response, advice and dedication to make this book possible.

The beautiful pages were designed by Marilyn Hochstatter, who, with my editor, Christine Townsend, continued to invest long hours going over details to give *Embracing Child Art* the highest quality presentation possible. I wish to acknowledge and extend my sincere thanks and admiration to Mrs. Harriet Mayor Fulbright and Ashfaq Ishaq from the ICAF for contributions on behalf of children world wide and the ICAF. I found I have made countless friends in the process of writing this book, including George Bussinger of McCallister's Art Supplies, Jerri Stanyan of K-12 Gallery, Lynne Juarez of Tule Elk Park, the teachers and parents of Sherman Elementary, and Rooftop K-8 Alternative School. I especially appreciate the photography by Jay Jones, Don Felton and Elizabeth Heffernan that captures the reality of how important art is to children. A special thank you to my dear friends and family who parted with prize possessions and sent things across the miles without obligation. I also wish to extend special thanks to the families of my church who complied with all the release forms and requests, unconditionally. And I must thank my children who rallied support and encouragement on a daily basis. I sincerely thank Sakura, ColArt, and Sanford Corporation, for their generous support. These companies and those listed in the Resources section at the end of this book know firsthand the joy of creating—and make it possible for many of us. There are countless more that inspired, intended and participated, and as you discover these resources and others, I hope you will find friends to nurture your creative spirit.

-Barbara A. McGuire

Dedication

For you
I will give constant surprise that will change every time it
*   touches you,*
For you
I will give a rainbow of wishes that will never grow old,
For you
I will give an invisible voice to speak to all creatures,
For you
I will give a secret passageway for escaping your fears,
For you
I will give a roaring fountain of faith to embrace your spirit.
I will give you my art—
Because you believe in me.

—To my mother and father, Paul and Marian Moeller

Rooftop K-8 Alternative Elementary School.

Photo by Jay Jones. Jason G. and Madison L.

Table of Contents

Robert M., age 8.

Kids & Kites. Chicago Mayor's Office, sponsored by Colorific, Sanford Corporation.

Chapter Five

Ideas, Environment and Guidance 76

Chapter Six

Letting Go-and Having Fun 92

Chapter Seven

Stacey F., age 3.

Stacy F., Age 3.

Tim M., age 3.

Foreword

Back when my daughters were little girls, there were no day care centers where we lived, and no understanding of the importance of the arts in the education and development of children. Trapped all day every day with our incessantly curious "perpetual motion machines," a few friends and I formed a play group. Each of us took turns with all our 3 year olds, which meant that we were each free four mornings a week. Later, when our family had moved, I not only initiated a new group, but also began to write about the experience. As I studied preschoolers and the activities that stimulated them, it slowly became clear to me how important the arts are in the development of children, especially before they feel comfortable with reading and writing.

What a wonderful guide and aid Barbara McGuire's *Embracing Child Art* is during this period. The book explains, sometimes poetically and sometimes with great clarity on the basis of sound research and experience, the essential importance of art and art projects. It also gives clear directions for imaginative, interesting art projects that are as much fun for the parent or teacher as they are for the child. For me, it made a weekend with my grandchildren one of the best ever, and it led to even more ideas generated by the children themselves. It made me eager to begin a dialogue, to make this book an ongoing work of art in itself.

Enjoy *Embracing Child Art*. Read it, carry out its projects, develop your own ideas, and use it to understand your own children, to appreciate their inner thoughts and expressions through their artwork, and who knows—you might even find yourself creating on your own.

-Harriet Mayor Fulbright
Chairman of the Board of Directors
International Child Art Foundation

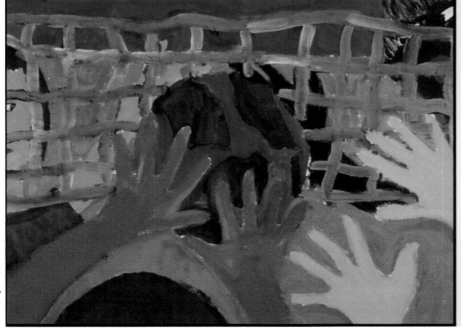

Kelli S., age 10, Louisiana.

the millennium - through a child's eyes

About ICAF and Art and Creativity

There is an amazing characteristic about art—it is always there for you. For me, art turned my world around when I was eight years old. My father died suddenly. Security, and life as we knew it, was shattered. I eventually found inspiration through the guidance of a young art teacher. She gave us the freedom to go beyond reproducing and actually create from our own imaginations. My paintings included many colors, people laughing, frolicking, and daydreaming. I was astounded and encouraged when my work was published and honored.

Years later, while studying at George Washington University in Washington, D.C., a children's festival on the National Mall inspired my ambition. I began to build the foundation for a national children's art organization. I realized that no such organization was in existence, nor was art being linked to creativity. Despite the growing importance of creativity in the global information age, children's art was not being used as a language-independent medium to promote global conscience and competence.

With the help of my wife and a few good friends, the non-profit organization, ICAF, was founded in 1997. Since that time, our festivals, exhibits, the *Child ART* magazine, and our ChildArt & Creativity Programs have blossomed into outreach involving over one million participants from eighty-six countries. Child artists, their parents, and teachers need no convincing about the importance of art, or the significance of ICAF. They understand instinctively. They refer to the magic of art and how freely they can express themselves, and how therapeutic and healing art can be. Our first *international* children's festival in 1999 included representation of children, teachers, and the first ladies from over fifty countries. Many of the children did not speak English and yet they were patient, making friends and communicating as artistically they could. They collaborated on a mural symbolizing their collective vision of the future. When children learn to create together they are unwilling to destroy what they or others have created.

We are grateful for the support from first ladies worldwide, including Mrs. Betty Ford and Mrs. Roslyn Carter. Artwork from ICAF has been presented in publications such as UNICEF, and the United States Department of Education, the Web sites of the UN Dialogue Among Civilizations, and the video productions of the National Park Service. This year, 2001, the Peter Drucker Foundation awarded me the Hesselbein Community Innovation Fellowship, and the Stockholm Challenge selected the ChildArt & Creativity Festival as finalists for its award for culture and entertainment.

ICAF is committed to children and the creativity of the future. This commitment is an investment in the minds and hearts and imaginings of children. We implore you to support and join ICAF so this global outreach of art can continue. Every donation makes possible the participation of children who cherish the opportunity.

Imagine yourself to be one of the children; creating a piece that may travel around the world. Imagine yourself in Washington at the 2003 ChildArt & Creativity Festival, the largest children's festival in the world. People are speaking all different languages, yet everyone seems to be communicating. You have high hopes about the world and everyone around you. You express your vision in your artwork. Your creativity blends with others and it is the most amazing experience of your life. And every time you see children create—you remember.

-Ashfaq Ishaq, Ph.D., FRSA
Executive Director, ICAF

Ashfaq with international child artists at ICAF's 1999 festival, ICAF.

I always wanted to be an artist.
Not just any artist;
A *good* artist.
I wanted acclaim.
I wanted acknowledgment.
I wanted recognition;
To be known as a really good artist,
So that I would always be admired.
So that my work would be admired.
Even though I was encouraged, I could never seem to get enough.
The praise was never assuring enough.
I could never believe it. I could not believe I was good enough.
I wanted to be such a good artist that I would never doubt my skill.
So good I couldn't be threatened by anyone disliking my art or doubting my skill.
I wanted proof.
I thought that if my art were good enough, it would allow me to be an artist.
It would allow me to be exceptional, unique.
I knew there is joy in creating.
There is fulfillment in creating.
There is closure in creating.
There is infinity in creating.
It took me forty-five years to realize that I had always been an artist.
A perfect artist.
And that being an artist had nothing to do with good art.
That being an artist had everything to do with being a person.
Being a person had everything to do with art.
That every child is an artist,
And art is being a child.

Alexis F., age 4.

This book is not designed to create graphic designers, Web page designers, product designers, fabric designers, filmmakers, singers, dancers, poets, actors, authors, or even artists.

This book will not threaten parents who cherish dreams that their child will become an engineer, a programmer, a doctor, a lawyer, a builder, a scientist, a teacher, a mail delivery person, an accountant, a nurse, or a big league baseball player. It will not threaten anyone who wants to become anything.

This book is designed to praise children. It is meant to capture a moment of their precious giving. It is designed to capture a moment of attention. It is designed to spark or create a memory of a single thought framed in time. It is meant to encourage, acknowledge, substantiate, and confirm that all children are artists, and that all children's art is good. Children's art is not to be judged; it is to be loved. If we can learn to be non-critical about something so pure, we can learn to put aside everything that means nothing. We can learn love.

Art of Every Child

When I first envisioned writing this book, I was well aware of the wealth of creativity residing in every home, every school, and every day care center. I was aware that even though my own children were of school age, I could still find children in day care that could create the same exquisite naive art that my children had created years ago. The well would never run dry.

My first question to many of my friends was "Did you save your children's art?" The answers ranged widely:

—"Yes, we have three of the those big tubs full of it in the basement."

—"We saved everything."

—"Most of it didn't last very long."

—"I think I have a few things—somewhere."

Some said specifically, "I have one drawing I keep on my desk that is the most precious thing in the world to me." One friend's mother informed me that even though her daughter was now forty-seven, she still had her art packed somewhere in storage; just thinking of it made her smile!

Child art is priceless. It only lasts a few years. It is as fleeting as childhood. I was panic-stricken when I thought my mother had thrown away some of my son's art. My son's childhood scribbles had been stuck between the good china—they were there for *safekeeping*. My mom had straightened things during a visit and after she left I noticed the drawings were gone. Panic ran through me.

Every child is capable of a masterpiece. Some children excel at certain things more than others. During one of the projects, I noticed that a young girl was having trouble coloring. The markers were smudging and her work was very undefined. It took a long time for her to complete just one piece. I didn't see much expression in her work. I was becoming *critical*. Then we moved on to the next project which was a fine ink pen drawing on tissue paper. She began to draw exceptional, incredible flowers. I was stunned and ashamed of my doubt. Her creativity blossomed through a different medium— simply changing from a marker to a pen made a world of difference.

Matthew H., age 5.

Photo by Marsha Lew. Amy L., age 5.

It is good for children to try all things. Eventually they will find something that they can really expand on. As adults, we cannot presume what choice that will be. Art is not predictable. Art is not gender-specific. Boys can weave. Girls can create with mud. When children are eight or nine years old, however, and are making bugs, you can't help but notice the gender generalizations. Girls tend to create butterflies and dragonflies, while scorpions and beetles typically populate the boys' art. The point is not to categorize or label the art but to simply appreciate whatever the child has to offer.

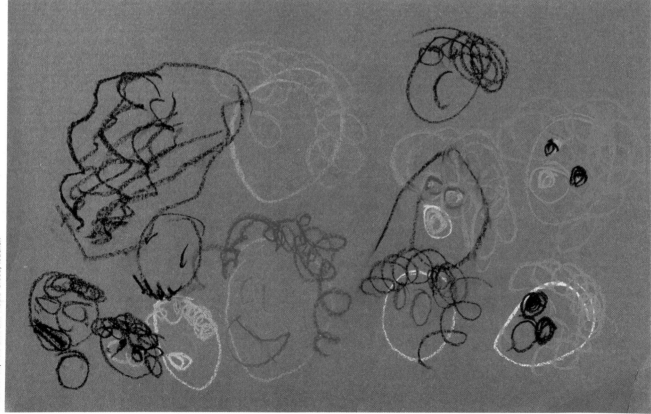

Indeed, child art is not something you can go into a store and buy. Sometimes while I was asking children if I could publish their art, I felt as if there was no way I could ever repay their precious generosity. I wanted to believe they wouldn't *miss* their art, but they kept asking, "Will we get the bugs back?" I realized that the children are connected to their art and concerned for its safekeeping.

The art in this book is not the best art I could find. The children are not exceptionally artistic children. Most of them are not children of artists; they're as "normal" as the kids on the block, nieces, nephews, you name it. Only one thing is tremendously special about these children. It's a thing that you can't see, a thing that you can't touch, but you can feel: the essence of the art. It's the heart behind it.

Andrew T., age 8.

Zachary G., age 11, Hanover Middle School, Sakura's Wonderful, Colorful World Contest. Theresa Grassle, teacher.

Charley K., age 5, drawing done at home, influenced by the movie, *The Iron Giant*.

Kimberley N., age 8, New Zealand.

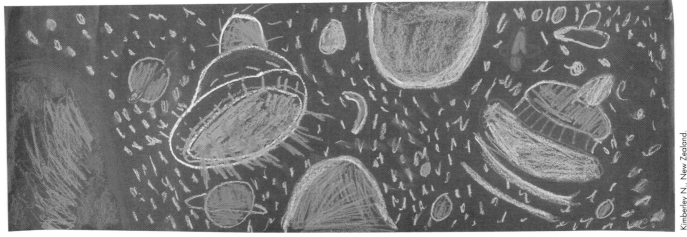

Kaitlyn F., age 11, "Liox," Grace Episcopal Day School, Sakura's Wonderful, Colorful World Contest. Kris Lesak, teacher.

Lauren H., age 7, Grace Episcopal Day School, Sakura's Wonderful, Colorful World Contest. Kris Lesak, teacher.

Contests & auctions

Some of the incredible art shown throughout the book is the result of entries in the Wonderful, Colorful World art contest sponsored by Sakura, Sanford Corporation, which manufactures Cray-Pas oil pastels, Gelly Roll pens, and other drawing and writing pens and inks. Sakura's focus is on color and personal expression. Their products are innovative and are of exceptional quality. I was overwhelmed at the opportunity to include some of the art submitted by 17,000 children for the 2001 coloring/drawing contest advertised to teachers and parents in *School Arts* and *Arts and Activities* magazines. Just gazing through boxes of children's art was an impacting education. It was obvious that some of the parents could not bear to part with the original art; they had submitted color copies.

I thought about these children who had not won first place, and what they would think about seeing their art in a book. Even though it had not reached the intended goal, the result was that it would be enjoyed and appreciated, perhaps even more than the winners' art would be.

I remembered my own thoughts about contests and being viewed, how many persons had actually seen and considered my entry, winning or not, and if my parents took note.

I remember pondering if I should even submit an entry, just for the sake of participation, knowing I could never win. I also remember winning, and how that picture of me receiving an award still rests in my book of achievements.

I spoke to Sakura's marketing director, Donna Wilson. As I was expressing my gratitude, she also extended gratitude that the children's art would continue to be appreciated. She mentioned that for young children, winning a poster contest could impact the course of their lives, change attitudes, and encourage esteem. As I said goodbye, it occurred to me that with art, every time you participate, you win.

Chapter One

The Beauty of Innate Creation

Photo by Jay Jones. Madison L. creates a rainbow.

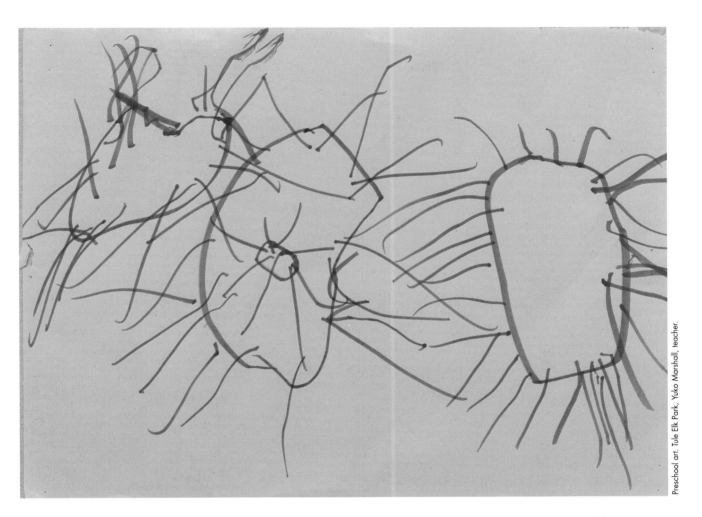

Preschool art. Tule Elk Park, Yuko Marshall, teacher.

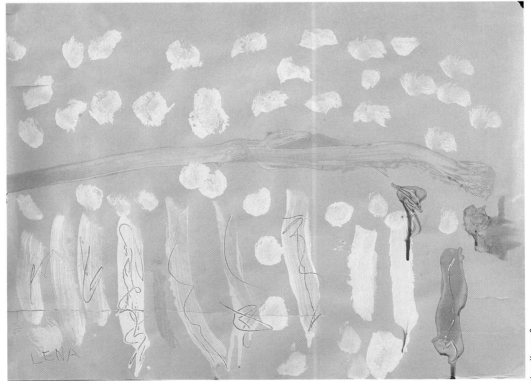

Lena K., age 3.

The Beauty of Innate Creation

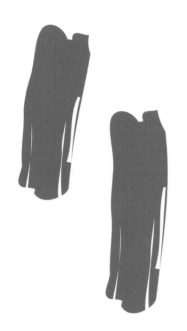

All the pieces in this book were possible because someone really cared to create. Someone cared to share. Someone went out of his or her way to participate. That's what they have in common. Whether they are from Cyprus, China, Romania, or next door, for a short while these children parted with their precious pictures, just for you.

There's no question in my mind whether children's art is actually art. This may be a personal opinion swayed by a love of creation, but this is a conviction to which I firmly hold. It has been said in some scholarly discussions that child art does not qualify as genuine art due to children's lack of control, intention, motivation, and deliberation in the creation. It has been posited that any aesthetic value we perceive in children's drawings is no more than a happy accident.

I do not wish to discuss what art is to scholars, critics, authors, and psychologists. I have great respect for the many who have dared to define art in their search for truth. But in this case, I believe we must not miss the forest for the trees.

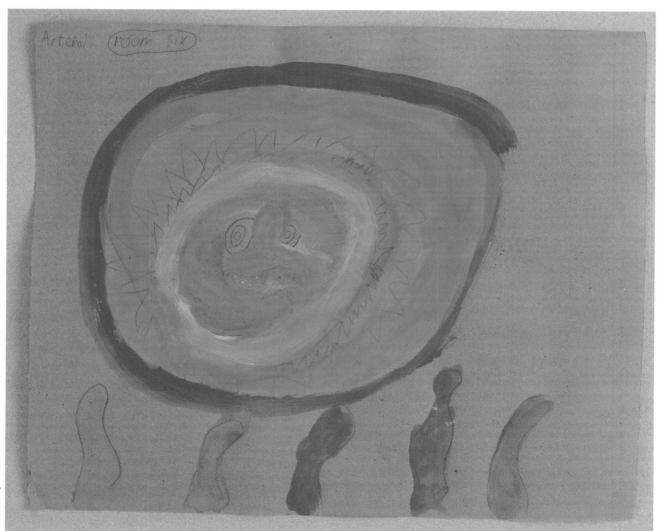

Artemi S., age 7, Tule Elk Park. Nuala Creed, teacher.

I stand to embrace child art as the purest form of art. Child art is about a process, is completely without intention, is not finished goods, not for sale, not for appraisal, not for decoration, and not for purpose. It simply is. It is creation. Child art is pure, and it is that purity that makes it beautiful. It is the only expression possible. There are no alternatives. It is complete and perfect. Nature is not to be judged and neither is child art.

Children eventually loose this purity of process. They lose the reckless abandon of creation. The will overtakes the spirit and the energy that previously flew forth without restraint. One can readily see the effects of the adult world upon the creativity of children once they begin to conform to adult expectations concerning art. Their art then becomes more realistic, and also more vulnerable to adult expectations, interpretation, and judgment. The art becomes more willing to please.

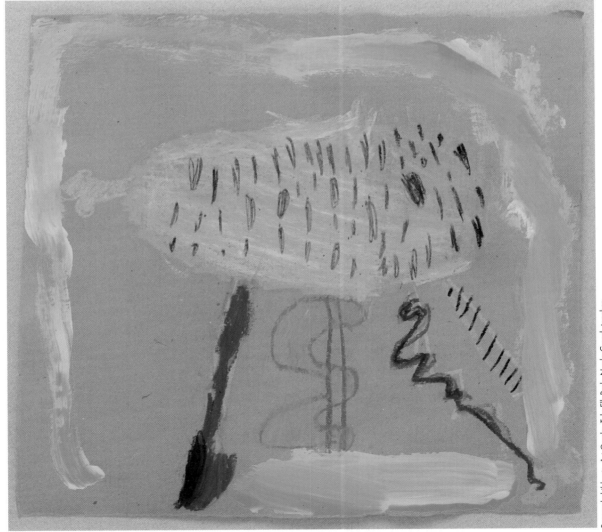

Rescued child art , 1st Grade, Tule Elk Park, Nuala Creed, teacher.

Is it no longer art, then? It is still an act of creation, but it is no longer pure. It brings with it the baggage of the world. It invites the interaction of the world. This art is no longer simply a vehicle for creation; it is the result of a tamed, curbed, and controlled spirit. It is a different kind of art that is determined to appeal aesthetically rather than for its pure energy. I find it hypocritical that we should encourage creative freedom, yet so severely limit creativity. I believe the creations of a maturing child or adult again return to being art when the person is able to reconnect with that original purity of expression and energy.

It is my goal to capture that special time when the art is uniquely pure—when it is in the first process of creation. Art is the first tactile and recorded material communication of a child. This creation is the one thing that can be captured or recorded simply because it is put into material form. You cannot save a first step; you cannot save the first word. In the unlikely event that either of these landmark developments could be caught on film, the action still lacks the material form and aesthetic presentation of language or communication displayed in art.

Jessica L., age 5, "Fairy Tales," Boulder Jewish Day School, Sakura's Wonderful, Colorful World Contest. Amy Yarborough, teacher.

Speaking solely from a position of observation and deep, spiritual receptivity, I dare to challenge scholarly discussions as to whether art must be controlled, intended, and mastered to be art. I acknowledge children as artists—the purest and greatest artists that we will ever be acquainted with in our lives.

Art for young children in school has often been taken for granted, and it is the first thing that we deem non-essential for their personal wholeness. It is usually regarded as an "extra" activity. Yet, many parents and educators are realizing that art is essential, necessary, and beneficial to academic learning. Educators today are striving to re-incorporate arts into the educational system as a fundamental necessity for learning—not just a playtime.*

Indeed, I also support the firm belief that art is essential to the development of thought processes, social interaction and communication. Creativity nourishes the natural and spiritual well-being of a child, and should not be suppressed or disregarded. It is as important and natural as physical exercise.

See current publications from the United States Department of Education, National Endowment for the Arts.

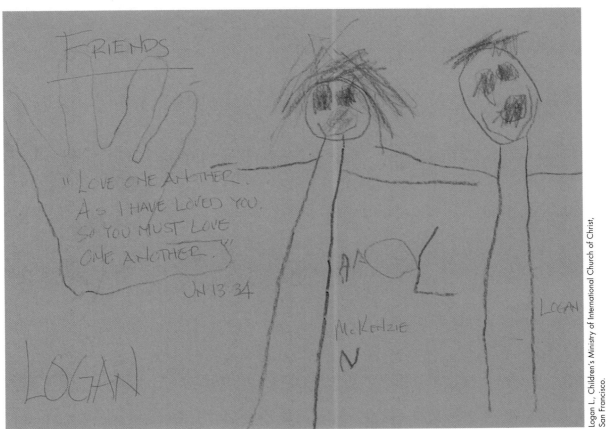

Logan L., Children's Ministry of International Church of Christ, San Francisco.

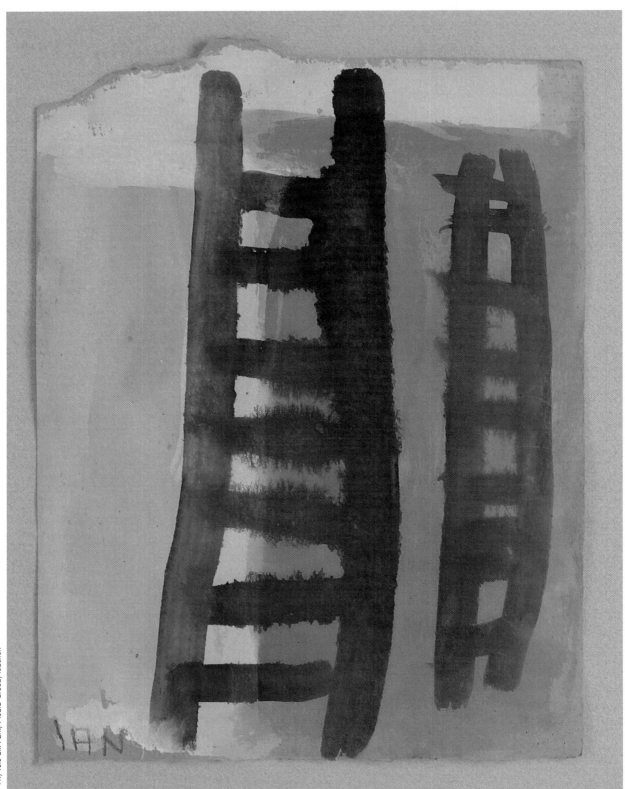

Ian W., Tule Elk Park, Nuala Creed, teacher.

When children have an opportunity to experiment with clay, watercolor, natural materials, light, color, wire, and all of the varieties of artistic media, over time, they develop a competence in using these languages to express complex emotions, ideas, and imaginings. The early childhood educators in Reggio Emilia, Italy, call this the "One hundred languages" of children. Teaching the children creativity and the ability to use art as expression is similar to teaching the "grammar" of a language. Particularly in an environment where the children are quite young or perhaps do not share a common nationality or spoken language, art becomes the universal common ground.

Lynne Juarez

Director,

Tule Elk Park Child Development Center

Sophia V., age 5. "Race Car #6."

Chapter Two

The Silent and Cognitive Communication of Child Art

Photo by Jay Jones. Alexander W., age 9.

believe that art is a basis for learning skills of organization, cooperation, problem solving, focus, and refinement. It lays the groundwork for developing patience, perseverance, determination, and respect.

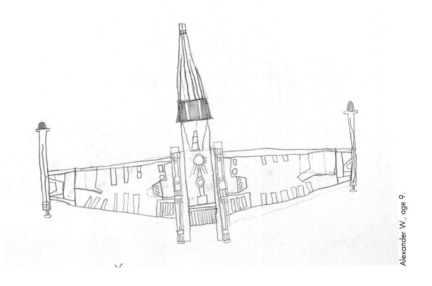

Alexander W., age 9.

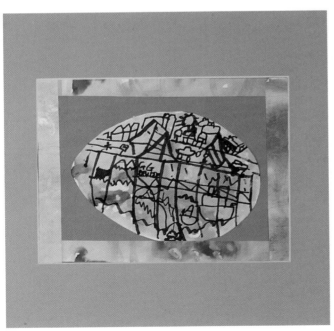

Easter Art Promotion, Sherman Elementary School, Pat Forte, Principal. Sponsored by Union St. Merchant's Association.

Art and the Natural World

The first attempts children can make in learning to differentiate involve their developing awareness of the ranges of size and color.

Repetition and grouping is an attempt to recognize and understand quantity. Art has an underlying relation to science and mathematics. A flower is usually drawn with more than one petal, and a child can recognize a multiple when drawing flowers and leaves.

Many children's drawings illustrate the scientific concepts of balance and gravity. A child may initially draw a house that is leaning to one side, but as the child matures, he will realize that the house must be straight to prevent it from falling down—it adheres to the basic rules of gravity. A tree is drawn

with a trunk and leaves. The tree must support the branches and the leaves. Eventually a child will draw a tree in this respect. He can use his drawings to interpret and work out his grasp of this concept. In a child's drawings, the sun is usually placed at the top of the page. It is easy to assume, then, that the child has not only observed this stellar fact and records it, but also that she understands that the sun gives light and warmth, and helps things to grow. Art is her first communication that she understands that concept, or at least trusts and represents it.

Similar understanding and communication is seen in children's drawings of the weather. Rain, pelting down from the sky or coming directly from a cloud, in children's drawings illustrates that they can communicate the happenings of the world around them, and that these occurrences have a natural sense of order. None of the above examples result from discussions regarding abstractions a child must visualize to grasp. They are basic, natural concepts that children exemplify through art.

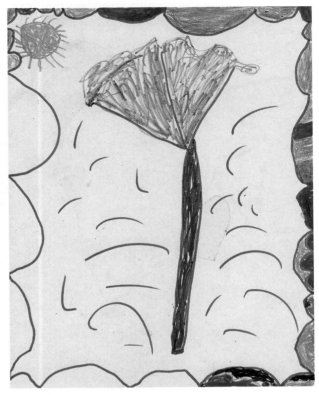

Haley S., age 3.

Rescued child art, "Chinese New Year," Sherman Elementary, from Jean Pong's kindergarten class.

Art and Communication

Much of our ability to express feelings and relate to others has a foundation in art and the physical means it provides for us to communicate. We began with the basic concept of expression. Art is the most immediate form for a child to represent an idea in communication that is nonverbal, even if the child is able to speak. A child's drawings reflect issues of importance to the child. This perhaps can be illustrated in the themes that are common to children's art, such as super-heroes for boys or horses for girls. The art is a vehicle for the child to experience and relate the power of the super-hero. Children draw pets to communicate their love of an animal. Howard Gardner reports, in his book about children's art,

Such drawings can allow the child to explore in his own ways, themes, and traits that weigh heavily on his consciousness. From a formal point of view the drawings spawn a rapid increase in the child's knowledge of spatial arrangements: in scarcely a year he moves from simple tadpole-like figures to forms sufficiently differentiated to allow easy recognition of a spate of fictional characters; he makes a transition from a simple lineup of characters to the beginning of genuine scenes; and he shows an incipient capacity to portray inner action among characters, conflict among forces, and the expressions of certain heightened motions. (Artful Scribbles)

Ghosts are out on coast making footprints everywhere. Every ghost is running because they are real ghost. Burple the footprint hunter is following the footprints. And back of him, there's another man following.

Kevin L, age 4, Tule Elk Park, Yuko Marshall, teacher.

In another discussion about a poem and drawing by his daughter, Gardner states, "Taken together, the poem and its illustration signify how a child can express to others in a form more effective than normal discourse her thoughts about a treasured experience in life."

The very emotional state of art is also an extraordinary tool for communication. Basic feelings such as happiness, sadness, gladness, fear, or embarrassment can be communicated through art. A child will very definitely draw a smile or a frown. This is reflective of the feelings of the characters in the child's story. Often the parents are drawn fighting or a family member is drawn detached from the family group. These are all expressions of the child's reality, communicating what a young child cannot put into speech. In many such cases, the art has more impact than direct verbal communication. Their art cannot be forgotten. It cannot be denied. The pictures can be taken literally or they can be discussed—but surely need to be acknowledged. Art is a very powerful tool in revealing the inner world of a child.

Another subtly profound learning experience through art is that communication is not always obvious. What the artist communicates is not necessarily what the viewer grasps; perhaps the viewer has no idea what the artist is representing. Further explanation and discussion is necessary to discover and understand what is being communicated. In other words, what you see is not always what you *think* it is! What you see may not always be the truth—it can be reflective of the imagination. Art is a tool that can communicate both truth and imagination.

Tatianna D., Sherman Elementary School. Laura Addario, teacher.

I asked my good friend, Leigh Edwards, whose children have special needs associated with their autism, to describe her children's art. Her observation not only substantiates the imagination present in all children, but also confirms, through their art, a world that is unique to them:

"It was fascinating to watch the kids sit on opposite sides of the table and 'do' their art. Brendon approached his with all the concentration of an engineer. He used only one color, and, if the paper was not big enough to accommodate the tail or neck of his dinosaur, he simply made it fit by making the tail swirly.

'On the other side of the table Brianna was swooshing colors onto her paper with gay abandon. Her favorite thing in life is a rainbow; naming the colors was one of the first things she ever did. She can name all ninety-six colors in the giant box of crayons! Her people drawings are fascinating, too. The first thing you'll notice is none of them have hands, but the shoes are given great detail with laces and a heel section. The shirts all must have collars and be left white (at least on Brianna's self portraits). She is very particular about the colors and simply could not go on when she discovered Brendon was using the particular shade of blue she wanted: there would be no substitutes——it had to be that color.

'On the family drawing she has drawn those of whom she would like to have back in her family. The two little ones are the children of a nanny we had. The baby was born while they were living with us and they left when she was about 2 months old, so Brianna's experience of Baby Katie was that she was always asleep, so her eyes are closed in the drawing. Still, no one has hands . . . I wonder why?"

Leigh Edwards

Brianna E., age 12.

Brianna E., age 12.

Brendan E., age 9.

Art, the Individual, and Society

We strive to teach our children cooperation. When it comes to art, materials must usually be shared, and this is an excellent opportunity to teach children how to be patient and considerate, as well as the concept of sharing. It is also necessary to teach them that if materials are squandered or tools are damaged, they will not have access to these things at a future time. Parents need to teach their children respect for others and their property. Art is an appropriate lesson for this principle at an early age. You can teach a child respect for their own work by signing and identifying their work, whereby they acknowledge, accept, and own the work that they have done. You can also teach them to respect others' works by not damaging or disregarding it. This teaches basic respect for a person's property and efforts. It is also teaching a respect for ideas, expressions, and creativity itself.

Art introduces opinion and attitude. A child may exhibit approval or disapproval of his own work, or the work of others. He may choose to comment on the creative

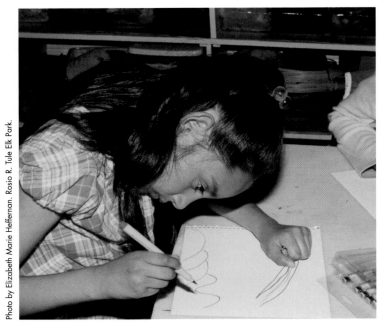

Photo by Elizabeth Marie Heffernan. Rosio R. Tule Elk Park.

Sara S., age 5 "My Cat," Salcha Elementary School, Sakura's Wonderful, Colorful World Contest. Mrs. Schlumbohm, teacher.

experience itself, his likes and dislikes about the material or subject matter, likes and dislikes about other people's works. He can also be taught to take others' expressions at face value and not criticize their work. Since there is no right or wrong in art, it is an excellent way to teach children acceptance and respect for individual preference.

Art is about making choices that are beneficial to the goal. You can teach a child to make choices independently, and do so with confidence, as well as convey the consequences of inappropriate choices. When you do, you are giving her much more than playtime.

It would be a mistake to underestimate the value of arts in teaching a child how to read and write. Mastering the pencil or pen, and following a set series of marks on a piece of paper to communicate a language, are fundamental to the structure of our society. The more practice a child has had

Phot by Jay Jones. Jason and Madison.

Samantha Y., age 6, Pinecrest School Northridge, "Little Dolphin Kissing Mama," Sakura's Wonderful, Colorful World Contest. Kim Culhane, teacher.

putting pen to paper, the more sense of familiarity he will have with developing the written word. The child who has control of a crayon will have more practice in controlling a pencil when he is taught to print. Later, when he is taught to write, artistic principles such as rhythm, unity, and movement are immensely valuable.

A child can learn rhythm by drawing waves on a lake; he can learn movement by drawing arrows or the trail of a bumblebee or a path through a town. He can learn unity by grouping all the flowers in the garden or all the stars in a sky. He can relate groups of objects to each other much the way groups of letters make a word. The unity reflective in a picture is parallel to the unity of characters in a story. The emphasis of a picture is parallel to the emphasis in a story. Art is a natural and indispensable gift for development, association, differentiation, and relation of objects to and among each other.

As I began to study the elements and principles of design, I became more and more aware of the necessity for an art foundation in education. Art is not merely a time to allow children to draw, paint, and have fun. Rather, art is an essential tool we must equip children with to help them understand how life works. For example, I realized that lines represent basic rules of organization within our society. Lines in the road keep cars from crashing into each other. Lines in grocery stores encourage cooperation and efficiency. We find food in the stores based on an organizational presentation. Shapes communicate traffic directions. Arrows indicate direction. Indeed we live in a world of icons where communication is often made through pictures.

First grade, Good Shepard Lutheran School. "Literary Quilt," Carol Wise, teacher, Elizabeth Heffernan, parent volunteer.

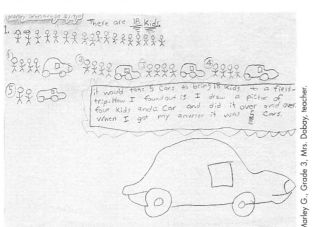

Denise C., Grade 3, Mrs. Dobay, teacher.

Lealoa N., Grade 3, Mrs. Dobay, teacher.

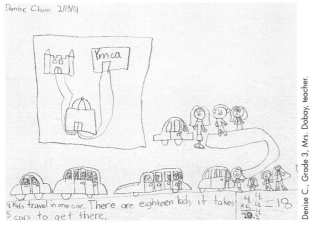

Marley G., Grade 3, Mrs. Dobay, teacher.

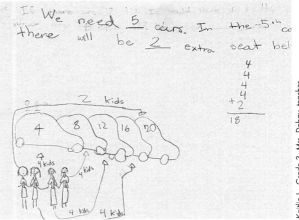

Kaitlin L., Grade 3, Mrs. Dobay, teacher.

First grade, Rooftop K–8 Alternative Elementary School, parent volunteers and supporters Dave Tegeda, Jude Deckenbach.

Colors are also an important means of communication in our society: green, a signal for go; red, a signal for stop. Learning to differentiate among colors is a significant skill for children to master, and as fundamental as the ABC's. But why do we abandon this foundation? I believe it is simply because we don't recognize its inherent value.

Nurture your child's art. Participate in child art activities and volunteer to help facilitate art in schools and community centers. Help bring forth the myriad benefits to be had by children experiencing creativity.

Caroline Zidek, teacher; poet, Gail Newman. Project sponsored by a grant from the San Francisco Art Commission.

Kids & Kites Event, Mayor's Office, Chicago. Sponsored by Colorific, Sanford Corporation.

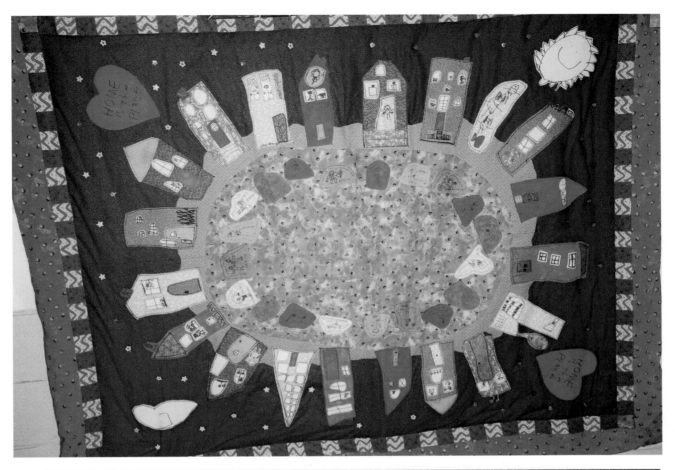

Kindergarten, Rooftop K-8 Alternative Elementary School. "House Quilt," image transfer and assemblage led by parent volunteers.

Embracing Child Art

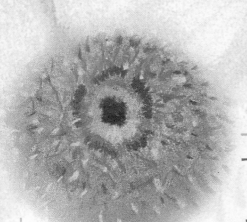

The Merit of Art

I always say I was a 4-H kid. The truth is that I was involved in so many childhood clubs (Bluebirds, Brownies, Girl Scouts, 4-H) that I got them all confused and can't remember when one stopped and the other started. I do remember that all of them afforded the opportunity to be creative. I remember the badges and the merit of accomplishment. You can get a badge just for learning about your particular interest. These clubs are the community playgrounds of the world, where nature and cultures and lifestyles are integrated and experienced and expressed through service and achievement. Everywhere, somewhere, there is a club or group that is doing art. Every county fair reflects creativity, effort, and achievement. The youth Arts Festivals that are held throughout the country each spring is a result of the National Art Education's Board to encourage a showing of creativity in our schools and communities. Many schools have a parent-run art program. School fundraisers often feature a cooperative effort between parents and classrooms to produce exceptional art, quilts, and painted furniture that in many respects is priceless. It is my hope that these activities will grow to the extent that they provide as much interest, entertainment, and enjoyment as cultural events in an adult world.

Chapter Three

Developing, Building, and Nurturing Through Child Art

Photo by Elizabeth Heffernan. Ausha W., age 7.

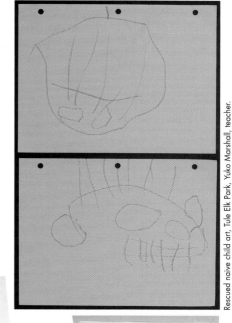
Rescued naive child art, Tule Elk Park, Yuko Marshall, teacher.

uring the course of observing both of my sons' artwork, I noticed an amazing similarity. Their personalities could not be more opposite, but at times I could not tell their work apart. A short time later, I came across art of my friend's child and it looked just like the scribbles of my own children!

It was then that I began to research if indeed this occurrence was real, not circumstance and not imagined. I discovered two books by Rhoda Kellogg: *Analyzing Child Art* and *The Psychology of Child Art*. Rhoda Kellogg has collected children's art for most of her life and had organized San Francisco's first nursery school in 1928. She wrote five books on the topic of child art, and drew her conclusions from over one million works of children in over thirty countries. I am completely indebted to Ms. Kellogg for much of what I write in this chapter.

But what was most compelling to me was that she scientifically substantiated what I had only casually observed in a few works. We cannot ignore that, worldwide, children's work bears distinct similarities. Through Ms. Kellogg's research, I learned that all children, regardless of race, ethnic background, creed, country or parents, developed drawing skills in the same fashion. There also appeared to be no differential in time. In other words, we have developed, artistically, in the same ways as our ancestors.

My Papa (Papa has his left hand in his pants)

Kimberly N., age 3, Matthew N., age 3, New Zealand.

Rynan N., Tule Elk Park.

Kasey K., age 3.

Ms. Kellogg states: "The artistic impulse is universal, as strong among the children of Korea or Spain or Siam as it is among the children of the Americas." Moreover, Ms. Kellogg's research pointed the way to the exciting discovery that "all children everywhere draw the same things in the same way at the same age."[1]

Due to the enormous amount of research she conducted over a long period of time, I choose to specifically acknowledge Ms. Kellogg as an unquestionable authority on the subject of children's art. I also find in Ms. Kellogg's presentations a deep respect and abiding love for the work of children, with which I personally can identify. Although she is not the only scholar to identify children's stages of artistic development and expression, it is clear that, based on Ms. Kellogg's findings, development in children occurs in the following fashion.

Children begin to scribble at about age two. It is a natural inclination; the child does not need to be prodded to perform the task of scribbling. Supplied with paper and crayon, a child will create marks. I remember that my own children simply pounded the paper with crayons, over and over again doing the same thing with a new piece of paper. I have witnessed children continuing to repeat the same set of scribbles, particular to each child. Ms. Kellogg explains this as a "primitive sense of figure-ground relationships."

Eventually a child's scribbles become shapes. The scribble is filled in, or repeated, or drawn over on the same spot. These aren't shapes like adults understand shapes. They are not outlined, but there is a definition between the scribble and surrounding space.

These bodies of scribbles eventually develop into an outline. The lines overlap or connect. They cross, they group, and nest together. The shapes and outlines are amazing reflections of the imagination of the child. There are no "expectations" of the drawings. They are pure discovery, but also a personal reference for the child to absorb. A child will adopt a scribble that he has made repeatedly, and this familiarity with his own work builds his

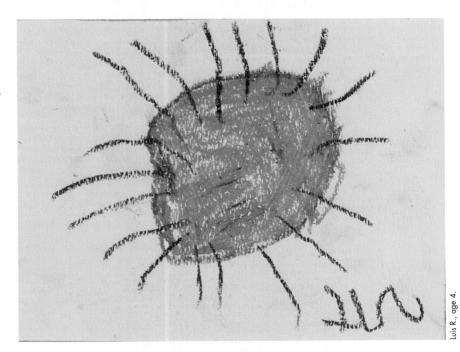

Luis R., age 4.

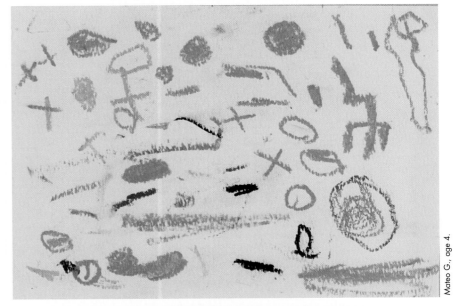

Mateo G., age 4.

Madison L., age 4.

Matthew H., age 4.

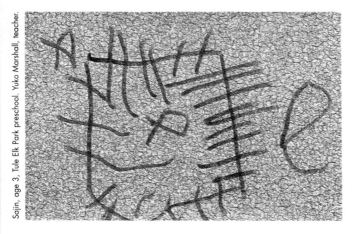

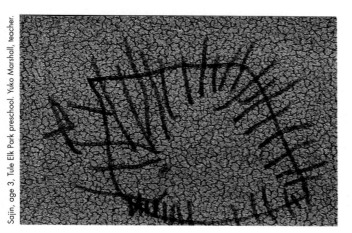

knowledge to discover and add more information to his experiences so he can draw on his learning for future delivery.

One of the earliest developments of children's art is the expression of balance. Spokes or shapes will be drawn to balance the work. These lines have no intended representation. They are just lines and shapes, but often they are reflective of what "looks and feels right" to the child. As human beings, we have a natural attraction to balance. Something that is not balanced emits an uneasy sense. Looking back at my children's work, I am amazed at the innate sense of balance I see in the early drawings. I am also amazed that boys' and girls' art in the early years is much the same. The pictorial development emerges in stages that are not gender related.

One of the most common and recognizable images found in children's art is that of the mandala. A mandala is a circle, crossed or nested. It is seen throughout ancient times as a symbol connected with spiritual expression and meditation, reflection, centering, beginning, and life energy. Mandalas have an undeniable quality of balance. The mandalas that a child draws eventually develop into suns, flowers, bugs, stars, and faces.

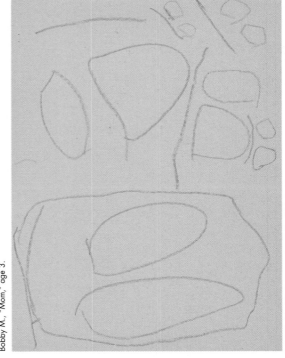

The human face is the most familiar and attractive image in a human environment. It is the recognizable feature of survival—another human being. It is no wonder that the mandalas of early childhood transition into drawings of self, mother, and father. Again, balance plays an important roll. Ears, hair, and circles for hands or feet all portray a child's natural sense of balance. Even though the work has begun to be recognizable, it is still not intentionally representational. Accurate rendition is not an element of child art, but it can be an adult expectation. Adults who insist on realism in child art can completely destroy a child's natural interest in art.

Eventually the child will be more cognitive of what his art represents, and he will strive to use his art to tell a story or denote an experience. The developing dexterity of children aged five and six also accommodates the advancement of recognizable images. This is the point at which unconditional encouragement is necessary for the child to continue to be self-expressive and creative in a demanding and expectant world.

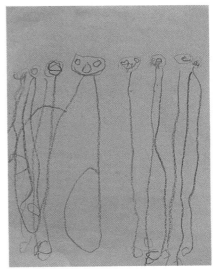

Luis R., age 3.

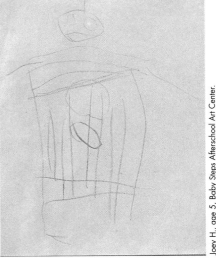

Joey H., age 5, Baby Steps Afterschool Art Center.

Robert M., kindergarten journal.

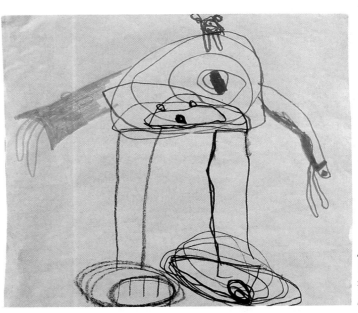

Ryan H., age 3.

What Is Creativity?

Creativity has been defined as the arrangement of pre-existing forms, objects, and facts in a new order by conceptual and emotional activity of the mind. The essence of creativity is to find a new thing and use it in a new way. Art offers a most valuable and enjoyable opportunity for expression of imagination, fantasy, emotions, and creativity. The urge to create is universal. During the preschool years this urge is likely to be intense, and the creative spirit inherent in every child needs to be encouraged if his or her free expression is to survive. By age seven or eight, the child's drawing may reflect the realism slowly permeating his thought, making him more like adults who lack spontaneity, imagination, and creativity——unless the danger is recognized and something is done to check the pull toward conformity.

Although their vision is direct, fresh, and personal, children's artwork during preschool years may not be looked upon as creative because the visual appeal of such artwork is often due to pure chance, not technical ability. Unfortunately, by the age of seven or eight, which has been referred to as the magic years or the flowering for child art, most children lose spontaneity and artistic creativity. (Source: J. H. Dileo, MD. *Child Development: Analysis and Synthesis*, Brunner/Mazel Publishers, NY, 1977.) This is often because of fundamental changes in the child's goals and orientation, the preference for words as a mode of self-expression and infusion of the need to reproduce exactly what they see and observe. Limits can be placed on children's creativity by an educational system that encourages imitation in learning rather than spontaneity and creative imagination. It is not enough to expose children to good art. They must make art if they are to benefit.

-The International Child Art Foundation

Maisy L., Tule Elk Park, Yuko Marshall, Teacher.

How Adults Can Help

Adults are the facilitators of creation. They are the suppliers. They are the organizers. They are the shepherds. They are the presenters. Adults are not the *source* of art—the source of art is the child. But the adults are the enablers. They are the leaders, the directors, the guides, the rulers, the dictators—*and* the nurturers.

The attitudes of adults are ever present in the development of the child. A child learns acceptance by response. A child learns judgment by reaction. A child learns doubt by rejection. An adult is extremely powerful in the building of a child. An adult is extremely responsible in the building of a child.

Photo by Don Tincher.

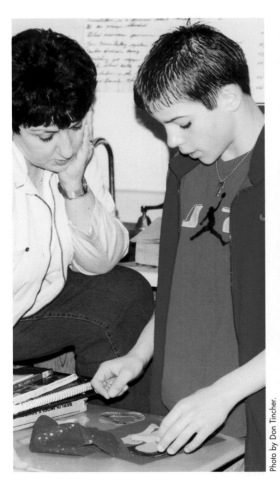

Photo by Don Tincher.

Photo by Don Tincher.

Adults are teachers, are they not? This book intends otherwise: that the child be the teacher and the adult be the child. The child is the facilitator, the leader, the director, the guide, the ruler, the dictator, and the nurturer of the creation. The creation is shared. The creation is facilitated, but it is unrestrained. The results are accepted. The results are marveled at and marvelous.

Once creation is unleashed and experienced, the adult is expected to return to an adult's stature and resume an adult skill. The adult is expected to complete the process with as much attention and skill as possible. The adult creates for keeps. Thus the project becomes the combination of best efforts, of both child and adult. The adult does not correct the child's work. The adult does not skimp or diminish. The adult embraces and cherishes the child's work.

A truly encouraging adult will frame and display the child's art. The expense, the time, the thought, the attention of a frame, all mean something to a child as well as to an adult. A frame is a blue ribbon. A frame is a parking spot. A frame is

a residence. A frame creates a home for art. A frame enhances. A frame accentuates value. There are many types of frames. A frame can be a pedestal. A frame can be a plate or a canvas. A frame can be a shelf, a wall, and a body. A frame showcases art. When art is seen, shown, displayed, worn, touched, and integrated into a home, it is felt. It is not a creation belonging to a person; it is the reflection of a person's creation.

There is nothing so impactful to young artists than to see their work framed. In this book, we will create many frames, many canvases, and many showcases. And hopefully the young artists will see and experience an appreciation for their work more powerful than what they can understand with words.

You can't buy esteem but you can invest in it every day. Esteem is a credit for acknowledging yourself as a valuable and cherished person. Encouraging esteem in your child by acknowledging her art is one of

Austin R., Grade 2, Gambert School. Teacher Laura Jicha.

John E., age 9.

Presentation

One of the best ways to preserve art is simply to frame it. This will keep it clean and intact. Use UV glass and hang the frame away from heat and light. Another suggestion is to take a scanned or digital image and store works electronically. Keep a portfolio handy to collect things brought home from day care or school. Be careful not to place items next to each other that will smear or bleed coloring. If a piece has exceptional quality but is on degradable material, such as newsprint, you may want to consider mounting it to a thin, woven-cotton cloth with a permanent spray adhesive. Laminating pieces will help to protect as well as accentuate the work. Spray varnishes may help to protect the work from being altered. Always test the finish and how it will react with the paper and the medium before applying it to the surface of your child's work.

Kindergarten art, Sherman Elementary, Jean Pong, teacher.

the first immediate, substantial, visual rewards that you can present a child. The child knows that she created the art. The child knows it is flawless, that it has no mistakes. It is valuable simply on the merit that it is her own art, and she is your child. The child knows that the parents or adults have distinguished this work from other accomplishments, such as picking up toys, or eating vegetables. The child knows that this acknowledgment is permanent. It will never diminish in greatness. The child is also satisfied and fulfilled. The art has completion. The child is drawn to produce more art, to continually nourish a need for acknowledgment and recognition. Words can be forgotten but the art is never out of sight.

We can accomplish this nurturing act simply by displaying the child art. Even if it is only a bulletin board, exhibiting their art establishes acknowledgment. There is, however, an incredible leap from the refrigerator to a frame hung on a wall. Child art really needs to be valued much like a photo, a painting, or any sort of desirable, beautiful thing.

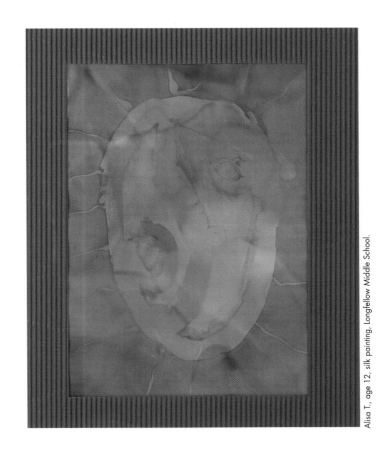

Alisa T., age 12, silk painting, Longfellow Middle School.

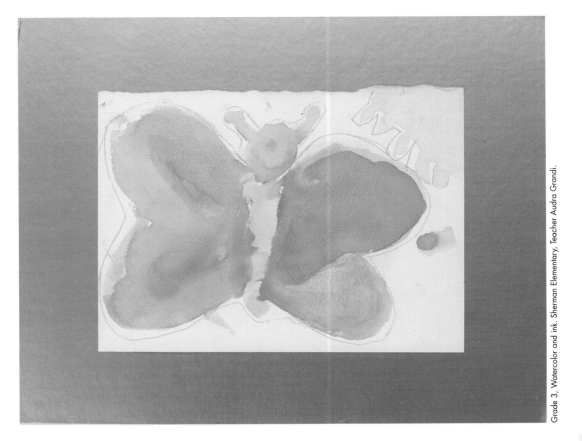

Grade 3, Watercolor and ink. Sherman Elementary, Teacher Audra Grandi.

Developing, Building, and Nurturing Through Child Art 51

Meilaysia C. K-12 Gallery for Young People, Dayton, Ohio.

Most adults are surrounded with things that make a statement about them. It is reflected in their choices of furniture, colors, decorations, books, and equipment. How wonderful that an adult can make a statement about how much child art is appreciated.

A child, too, can gain the security of things that reflect her life, such as her books, her toys, and her art. The art is the only thing actually created by the child. The art has the most intimate relation to the personality of the true child.

The projects in this book are suggested as ways to further embrace children's art beyond the refrigerator. There are ideas presented to bring children's art into everyday things, such as journals, pillows, and jewelry. It doesn't even need to be art produced by your own children. It is further substantiating to acknowledge the artworks of friends and classmates. It says the art is desirable even if it is not theirs. Children consider their art valuable when they create it for each other. It is truly a gift.

Once I came across a drawing I thought was my own child's. It was a picture of Superman and the "S" was written backward. I thought it was so charming I put time and effort into making a

"Superman," Luke L. Carved polymer plaque by Barbara A. McGuire. Children's Ministries, San Francisco International Church of Christ.

Matthew 18:3

"I tell you the truth, unless you change and become like little children, you will never enter the kingdom of heaven."

carved piece out of the image and framed it. At some point, my children informed me that it was their friend Luke's drawing. I was surprised they even knew whose it was. Admittedly, I was a little disappointed my own child had not created it, but I think the children seeing me put as much effort into someone else's art also acknowledged their friend's talents and deepened their respect for art in general. It was a good lesson not to be so centered on the limited world of only my own children, but to enjoy other children's art.

Skyler W. K-12 Gallery for Young People, Dayton, Ohio.

I recall, when I was collecting art for this book, the imploring eyes of one of the children at the after-school center. You could feel the longing for the work to be accepted. There was no way I could dismiss the intense attachment to the art, as if I were viewing the child herself. Each child wants to be counted.

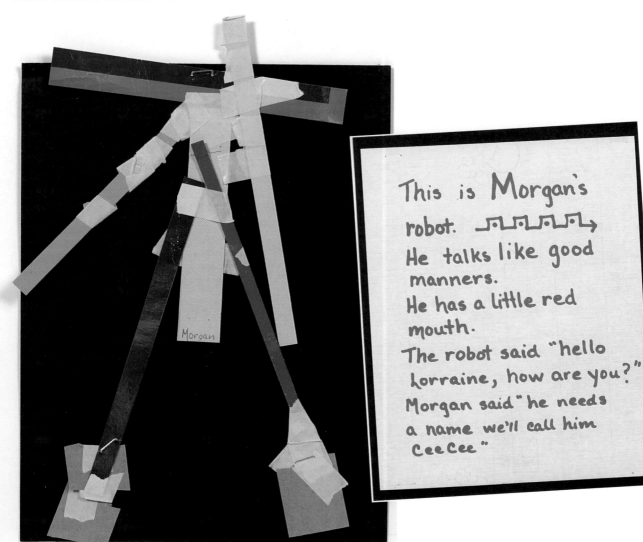

This is Morgan's robot. ⌐⌐⌐⌐⌐⌐⌐,
He talks like good manners.
He has a little red mouth.
The robot said "hello Lorraine, how are you?"
Morgan said "he needs a name we'll call him Cee Cee"

Morgan D., age 3.

Summer D., Duncan Ceramic Studio.

to dad love Summer xox 96

Khira B., Tule Elk Park, Brigid Haran, teacher.

Embracing Child Art

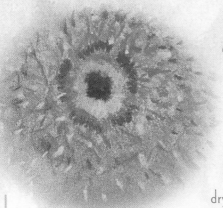

"Children really love to come to the Art Room. They become focused and absorbed in their creations. When I meet them outside the Art Room they inquire as to how their pieces are: 'Is my painting dry?' or 'Has my cup been fired?' They recognize their work and the work of their classmates. When they feel they have accomplished something, they take great pride in it. A few children have opted to leave their artwork at school. When I inquired why, I was told that their parents threw out their other artwork. One nine year-old who had made her first teapot and glazed it beautifully was told by her mother it was not good enough as it did not function well."

Comments from the children when asked why they like the Art Room:

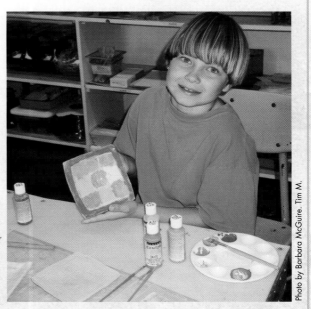

Photo by Barbara McGuire. Tim M.

"I like it because you get to make your own thing. I made a pillow."

"Kids get to do special activities they can't do in the classroom."

"It's a good place to help kids' minds grow. I made a clay skull."

"You get to do projects you might like."

"You learn a lot of things and have presents for Mother's Day."

"You can learn new things about art."

-Nuala Creed, Artist in Residence, Tule Elk Park Child Development Center, sponsored through a grant by the California Arts Council, along with funding from the San Francisco Education Fund and contributions from Bank of America.

Chapter Four

Elements and Principles

for Child Design

Photo by Jay Jones. Vaneka R., age 8.

The Aesthetics of Elements and Principles of Design

The subheading, above, hardly sounds like anything a child can comprehend. But actually the elements and principles of design make total sense in the order of the universe and actually are quite user-friendly. Once they are embedded into our means of expression, utilizing the elements and principles of design become a recipe for success. These terms are not limited to artists, designers, or scientists, but are everyday common things that are so natural that we take them for granted. In fact, they are so familiar we often do not even realize they are there.

I am going to introduce the elements and principles of design in simplistic terms intended to identify with children. There is much more to these concepts that invites further study. A great deal has already been written about the theory and structure of art. All children's art is great and some of it is successful in design quality. I am only going to point out a few secrets of design success. Success breeds success, so when repeated, not only are the good foundations of art supported, they are also rewarded.

Vanessa D., age 9.

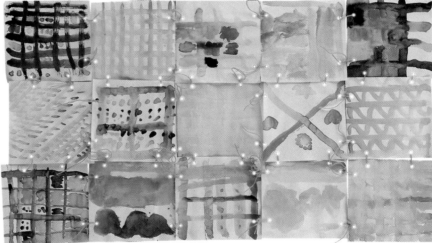

Group project. Kindergarten, Sherman Elementary. Jean Pong, teacher.

A.J. W., age 6. "Paint Truck Birds." Gloverville Elementary. Sakura's Wonderful, Colorful World Contest. Beth Teeters, teacher.

Elements of Design

We will start with the element having the biggest impact of all—color. Color is like a poker hand; you add and subtract until you have a hand that wins—colors that appeal. Usually there is one very different color that makes the predominant group stand out even more. When you are working with children, you may notice that

their choice of color seems random. The idea is to flow with their choices, and suggest colors that are in balance and do not compete with each other. If you are very purposeful in color because you wish to evoke a certain mood, *limit* the colors and let the children choose from a color group, such as pastels, or a certain quarter of the color wheel. An example of this would be to limit the palette to blues and greens, or perhaps reds and purples. Adding black and white to the mix will usually help to balance out any colors that are competing for attention.

Khira B., age 7. Tule Elk Center, Preschool. Nuala Creed, teacher.

Matthew K., age 7. "Is It Really What You Think It Is?" Tess Corners School, Sakura's Wonderful, Colorful World Contest. Claire Warnke, teacher.

Value

Value is just as effective as color, but in a more subtle way. Varying value adds immense depth to a work. In a child's world, value can be interpreted as "voices": a soft, medium, or loud voice, a high or low voice. It takes a whole group of voices to make a choir. Harmony is more than one voice, singing the same note. Light colors have a high value and dark colors have a low value. Try to use some of both, high and low value, even if they are of the same color.

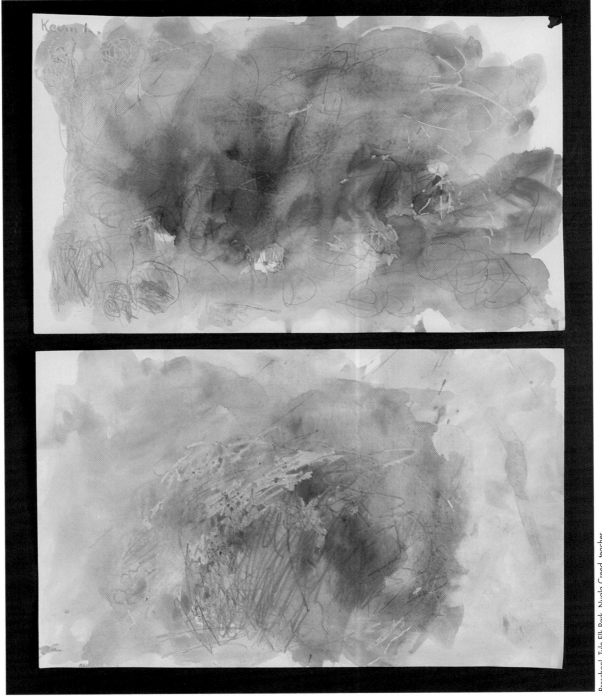

Preschool, Tule Elk Park, Nuala Creed, teacher.

Line

Everybody knows what a line is. A line is a mark. But a line can *move*. A line can point. It can rock and roll and twist and shout. It can split into a million pieces, in a million directions. It can contain things—and it can divide. Lines are the most important tools I know of for organization. Our entire written language is based, and successfully functions, because of lines and our respect for what they communicate. Lines are a great way to learn to differentiate details such as short and tall, thick and thin, straight and curvy.

Nicholas F., age 7, "The Dancing Bugs." Humann Elementary School, Sakura's Wonderful, Colorful World Contest. Natalie Parker, teacher.

Ian T., age 8, "The Spider." Humann Elementary School, Sakura's Wonderful, Colorful World Contest. Natalie Parker, teacher.

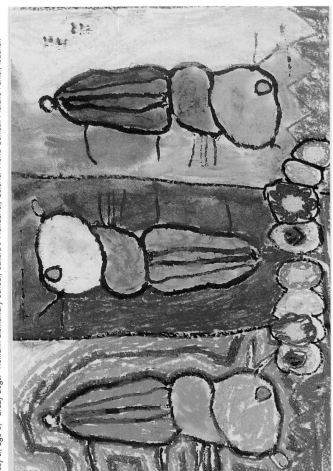

Lacey L., age 8, "Crazy Bugs." Humann Elementary School, Sakura's Wonderful, Colorful World Contest. Natalie Parker, teacher.

Shape

Shapes are cool! Way beyond ordinary circles, squares, and triangles, child art is the greatest shape show on earth. This is where the children are masters. Their shapes are imaginative, delightful, quirky, and so, so unique. Kids have shapes *down*.

Form

Form is akin to shape, only it's 3-D. Since most child art is not representative of volume and form, form is a concept that will emerge in later years. That said, child art entertains fearless form. Children are willing to make completely alien forms: a lump, a volcano, or enlarged, bulbous, beings of unnatural proportion. Most houses, humans, flowers, and dogs have only a front face, not a side or a back. Child art rarely casts shadows.

Braden H., age 7, Valley View School. Sakura's Wonderful, Colorful World Contest. Donna Beth Pierson, teacher.

Artemi, Tule Elk Park.

Andrew T., age 7.

Henri C., age 5, Napa Valley School.

Texture

Children excel at creating texture on a flat piece of paper—one of their favorite activities is to glue something on to it. That something could be sand, that something could be cotton, that something could be a sequin. All of these "effects" create a texture you can touch and feel. Then there are simulated textures: the mountains that actually look like they are rocky, the hairs that actually look prickly, clouds that actually look fluffy.

Space

Having a limited sense of ownership, children are naturally generous with space. They do not have a compulsion to fill it. The floating figures are simply present. In later years, space becomes associated with placement and relationship between objects. The sun is high in the sky with space between it and the Earth. The car or horse is flat along the bottom of the page, placed there to establish focus and gravity. Each figure is given its own space independently; they rarely overlap. The elements are related because they are in the same picture but the objects are not grouped, and their relationships are not always evident to the viewer.

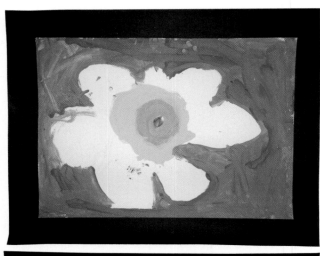
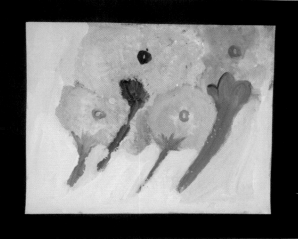
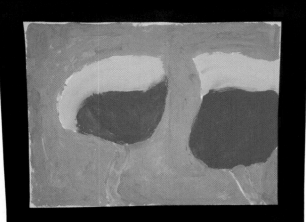

Principles of Design

This is where the lines, colors, and shapes combine to make sense. The principles of design are how the elements relate to one another, how the elements work together to make a composition.

Balance

Enlarged ears protruding from the head, arms extending from the head, or hats on earless faces—these all result from an innate sense of balance and a child's means of bringing this concept into his own reality. This is a child phenomenon. This type of art is incredibly beautiful because it defends logic and defies truth. Art is the extreme simplification of an object, and children have achieved this with perfection in the balanced figures of early childhood. Balance also encompasses symmetry, especially radial symmetry. The early mandala-like figures show an appreciation for balance that radiates from a center. Large eyes balance a face void of complex detail. Even at a young age, children usually draw two eyes, arms and ears. Are these representations of reality, or displays of balance?

Another display of balance is the occurrence of a very large area of space balancing the action and detail of a complex figure drawn to one side.

Kimra K., age 7, "Toucans," Esperanza School, Sakura's Wonderful, Colorful World Contest. Mrs. Todacheene, teacher.

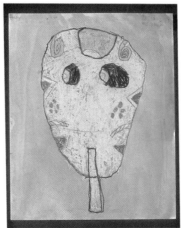

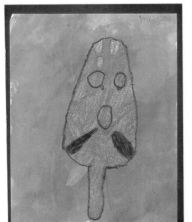

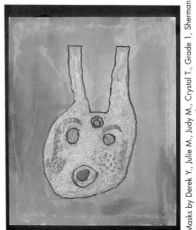

Masks by Derek Y., Julie M., Judy M., Crystal T., Grade 1, Sherman Elementary, Winnie Lee Leung, teacher.

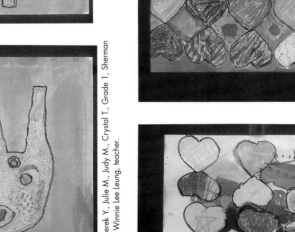

Kindergarten, Sherman Elementary, Jean Pong, teacher.

Pattern

Pattern is the duplication of shape, line or form that results in a larger design. The paper-cut snowflake is a good example of a pattern. When these designs are arranged on a grid, they evolve into a complete surface design or a border. Adults may be familiar with the concept of the "every other" pattern when making a border, but young children are not. I once did a pattern project with a group of kindergarten children. The instructions included decorating the frame border of a clay pin. I thought it was a simple project, but to my surprise, not all the children grasped the concept. I was shocked to discover that patterns are a learned concept. Apparently this is a young age for children to learn about sequences. It also surprised me that the children more accomplished in academics were not necessarily the first to understand the creation of a pattern.

Rhythm

The natural progression of a pattern produces rhythm. Rhythm is a sequence or the duplication of an object that creates eye movement. It is also the repetition of an object diminishing or enlarging in size to establish a special relationship or a size relationship. A good example of rhythm is the frond of a fern. The leaves at the bottom are larger and diminish as the frond develops to the tip of the plant. The placement of the individual leaves and the relationship in size creates a rhythm. Rhythm is a soothing and stabilizing design principle, most likely because it is inherent in nature. It can be utilized in art when we incorporate the "all in a row" concept of certain images, shapes, or lines. Three similarly framed pieces of art in a row is a classic, enduring interior decorating rhythm.

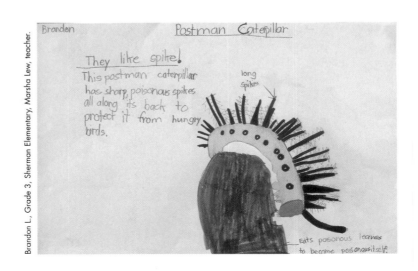

Contrast

Something that stands out draws attention. This can be done through grouping, or differentiating, with color, size, or shape. If you have four squares and a circle, the circle is in contrast and draws attention. Contrast is difference. It breaks the monotony. It catches the eye.

Emphasis

This is sometimes a hard thing to grasp because you want your entire picture to be noticed. But there should be some central thought or point that is being communicated. Placing an object in the middle of the page indicates emphasis on that object. Enlarged objects have emphasis. Repeating the color, or repeating the shape or image makes that object become the theme or focus of the work. When my son was four, all he drew were super-heroes. His drawings were simple figures suspended in air and quite undistinguishable except for the one thing they all possessed—an enlarged belt. This belt contained the identity of the character, and it was their source of power. This is important because if children can communicate emphasis through drawing, it is likely that they will be able to communicate it in later years through literature or speech. Emphasis causes us to focus on the information that is the most effective.

Jennifer A., age 6, "Down on the Farm." Panama Central School, Sakura's Wonderful, Colorful World Contest. Debbra Bailey, teacher.

Linda Kholobekian, age 6, Nigeria, ICAF.

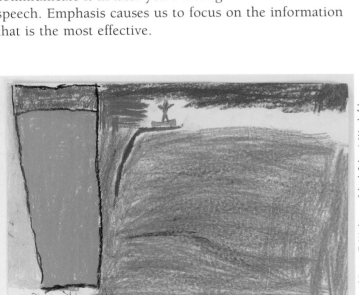

Richard S., age 7, Washington School, Sakura's Wonderful, Colorful World Contest. Catherine Dokachev, teacher.

Carly Rose D., age 8, "French Kitty Kat." OLPH School, Sakura's Wonderful, Colorful World Contest. Mrs. Ann Meinert, teacher.

Movement

Movement is the action in the art. It is the strategic placement of objects that draw attention to the entire composition. Movement can be seen in the lines that radiate outward and point in a direction. Rhythm also creates movement. A good experiment is to ask a child to draw arrows, or a maze that will lead the viewer to a certain object that is the focus of the drawing.

Unity

Unity is the grouping of things that have something in common. Unity is prevalent everywhere in society and is the basis for organization. My children used to play a computer game that taught differentiation between animals and plants, and also encouraged finding things that belong together, or unity. In a home, you would not find the blender in the living room; it doesn't belong there. In a story, all the characters relate to the plot. None are just there hanging out. This is also true in art. A watercolor shouldn't have a piece of construction paper glued to the middle of it. It would be out of place. If children are able to organize their art, to separate and distinguish what belongs, they will lay the foundation for organization and appropriate relationships to make their lives more efficient and productive, as well as eliminate stress and confusion.

It is a pleasure to see the elements and principles appear in children's art. Some kids do it naturally; others learn things gradually or by instruction. Some kids never pay attention and their art reflects total chaos. Art is a gift, but it is also a skill that we can grasp and utilize in communication. Art enables the imagination and brings vision into being.

Nora Skalleova, age 9, Czech Republic. ICAF.

Marki N., age 6, "Ballerinas."

Paige P., age 6, "Happy Face." Pinecrest School Northridge School, Sakura's Wonderful, Colorful World Contest. Stacy Palamara, teacher.

Elements and Principles for Child Design 67

Child Art and Colors

Children's colors are usually associated with the bright primaries, namely red, yellow, and blue. We don't even realize how much we force-feed these colors into our children's existence. Consider, too, how colors can be "genderized": pink is for girls and blue is for boys. When we categorize in this way, we are leaving out all possibility of imagination and individuality.

It is true that colors evoke emotional associations. Dark colors are intense and heavy. Pale colors are light and soft. Primaries are playful. De-saturated colors are rich and elegant. We associate babies with pale colors and toddlers with primaries. As adults, we rarely choose such bright colors. We prefer more subtle, complex colors, shades and tints, de-saturated designer colors … rusts, olives, and slate. Sometimes a child creates a masterpiece of color simply because she has mixed the colors in washing out the brush, adding a complexity to the hue, and beautiful, unique colors are achieved.

In encouraging children to create art, it is reasonable to allow them to select colors as they wish. It is also good to restrain from choosing colors for them. Children will find their way around a color box.

If they wish, it is acceptable for them to use black. Black is bold. Black is deep, intense and strong. For all practical purposes, a purple head is just as appealing as a yellow one. Practice, and comparisons made among their own works, will help children make decisions about color.

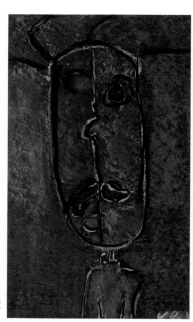

Eduardo E., age 9, "Colors of Light." Sawyer Elementary School, Sakura's Wonderful, Colorful World Contest. Anna Waywood, teacher.

Cameron B., age 8, "Picasso." Cobb School, Sakura's Wonderful, Colorful World Contest. Peggy Robertson, teacher.

Keli W., age 7, "Picasso." Cobb School, Sakura's Wonderful, Colorful World Contest. Peggy Robertson, teacher.

Shane T., age 7, "Picasso." Cobb School, Sakura's Wonderful, Colorful World Contest. Peggy Roberton, teacher.

But now, I am going to suggest something radical—that adults *do* actually make color choices for the child. When we do, we can still give the child choices within a group of possibilities, but we're not restricting their creativity. If adults dictate the color palette, and give children choices within that range, they can experience incredible results that will sophisticate the nature of the art. Why should we train children to choose red, yellow, and blue? Why not allow them to choose ochre, teal, and rust, olive, maroon, and khaki? They are too young to comprehend the recipe for producing sophisticated color. If choosing this palette for our children to create art produces a greater appreciation and fosters broader display, I feel the transition from primaries to complex colors is worth making.

Preschool child art, Tule Elk Park, Nuala Creed.

Thomas-Anthony V., age 6, "Rocky Hill School, Sakura's Wonderful, Colorful World Contest. Trixie Dumas, teacher.

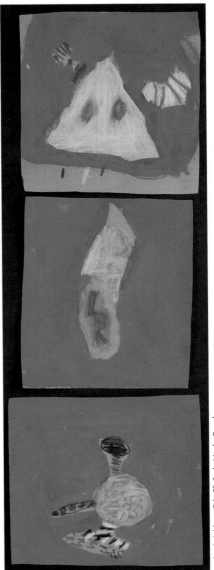

Preschool child art, Tule Elk Park, Nuala Creed.

Photo by Barbara McGuire. Joanne, Tule Elk Park.

Presumably, the primary colors are associated with children because the primaries are the building blocks of the entire range of conceivable color. This is a magnificent scientific phenomenon. But most people do not understand color mixing beyond the basic color wheel of red, orange, yellow, green, blue and purple.

I believe that children can develop a more complex understanding of color if they are allowed to experience color itself. In other words, children have a greater chance of understanding what makes golden brown if they are familiar with golden brown in the first place. I actually watched my son's classmate illustrate this, through watercolors, to his peers by showing them his "recipe" for golden brown. It was obvious that he was familiar with the color he was trying to mix. His friends were amazed and regarded him with high esteem.

Mixing color can also be an introduction to mathematics, as it is a good example of equations involving fractions. Equal portions of primary colors should produce secondary colors. Mixing lime green, teal blue, and fuchsia all represent the power of a fraction and illustrate proportions.

Shoe Box. Simon Z., Sherman Kindergarten, Jean Pong, teacher.

Teaching color is a sophisticated, but tricky lesson, because not all art materials are created with pure pigments. Nor are all materials created with the same saturation. Red can easily overpower a yellow. A good way to test the accuracy of the pigment and saturation is to mix equal parts of the primaries, red and yellow, yellow and blue, and blue and red. A perfect pigment balance will produce orange, green, and purple respectively.

Imbalanced primaries will not produce a true secondary. Polymer clay is an excellent medium to teach color because the children can see the color change in their hands. It is easy to measure so proportions can be duplicated or divided. Adding a bit of black can explain how a *shade* is made, and adding a bit of white can illustrate how a *tint* is made. Not only

Matt S., age 12. Cherish Rivas' Afterschool Program.

Summer D., Fresno, California.

is it good to recognize black and white as colors, but also to see the effect when adding those colors to each of the other colors. You then are not only teaching color, but also a design element called value, the light and dark properties of a color. This is another aspect of art you can teach children that will broaden their possibilities and sharpen their ability to distinguish and make choices.

Blank pages

Even though I love art, a blank page has always intimidated me. I consider it an amazing feat that a child can immediately jump into such an amount of white space with no fear of consequence. Often when children are very young, the mere consequence of putting the crayon to the paper and producing a visual mark is a magical experience. Children are mystified with the trail of color and line. After the fascination with scribbles, adults often try to make something recognizable of the art. Since the art doesn't look like anything familiar, the parent may feel prompted to teach.

At first, familiar shapes emerge such as circles, squares, triangles. Then a parent illustrates how to draw familiar things such as a sun, a flower, and a face. When the adult is drawing and the child is watching it is amazing to witness the mimicking.

If I sit down with five children and explain that we are going to make art with watercolor pencils, I first illustrate how the pencils work. I will begin with a line, a box, a circle, and many times, a spiral. I then change colors and eventually use the brush and water to wet and blend the color.

I am simply playing. Quite often the children will begin to mimic my illustration by choosing something I have drawn that they like. It may be they are mimicking an action more than the image, such as the swirly motion of creating a spiral. Sometimes they draw in exactly the same sequence. This type of mimicking is more complex. They build on what they have already accomplished and must retain the sequence in their memory.

Children are also intrigued by the application of new materials and tools. They love to use a brush. Application of the water and brush is a special and rare treat. The same is true for rollers if you are working with clay and winding tools when you are working with wire. Kids love the tools. Children enjoy the challenge of the manipulation of the tools and it is a great way to help develop their small motor skills.

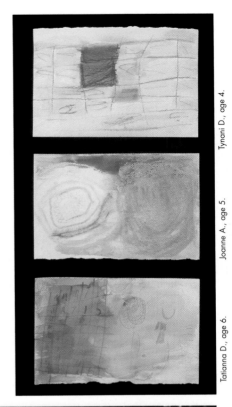

Tynani D., age 4.

Joanne A., age 5.

Tatianna D., age 6.

Tatianna D., drawing on Reynolds Bright Ideas foil.

Vanessa D., age 8.

Photo by Barbara McGuire. Tatianna D., and Georgina R.

Another thing they like to do is paste … paste, and paste, and *paste*. They paste things on top of things. You can choose to let them create independently or you can give them some alternatives by illustrating how to paste over the entire surface. This may be an initial challenge of wills, but showing them and telling them are two different things, and showing communicates more effectively. (Of course to do this, you need to create art as well as "dive right in.")

Eventually, you will want to encourage more than mimicking, and encourage the child to use her imagination. If the child is at a loss for ideas, or if the drawing should have a purposeful theme, you can encourage her creativity by making open-ended references. Allow the child to fill in the story you prompt them with:

Styro Prints, Tule Elk Park preschool, Nuala Creed, teacher.

Remember when we_____ ?
Remember that picture of_____ ?
Remember the color of _____ ?
What would a _____ look like?

In this way, you pull images from a child's own realm of familiar experiences.

Many times the child will have a complete story associated with a drawing. Expand on that theme. Create another drawing of a detail of the first drawing. Create a variation of the first drawing. Keep the child engaged for as long as possible. The child will learn to expand the imagination, and focus on the details of the expression.

Photo by Elizabeth Heffernan. Artemi S.

Vaneka R., age 8.

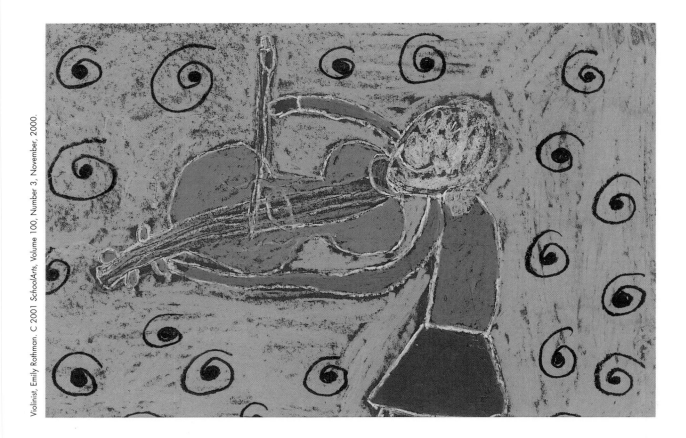

Violinist, Emily Rothman. C 2001 SchoolArts, Volume 100, Number 3, November, 2000.

Saxophone Player, Kateri Bisceglio. C 2001 SchoolArts, Volume 100, Number 3, November, 2000.

Dear Mrs. Thumbelina,
I think you are the nicest character
I have ever known. And I heard about
you and your stories. In fact! I have one of
your miniature books. Why are you so tiny?
Thumbelina you are the prettiest I have
ever seen, and you're the prettiest in the whole
world I think! Well that's mine and your opinion.
Did you play outside in the day time? I think
so but I may be wrong because I didn't
read it all of your story. Did you climb back
in your flower to sleep? Did you get
bought from the store? Did you play
with the dog and did you play hard so you're
tired when it's dark?

From

Laura

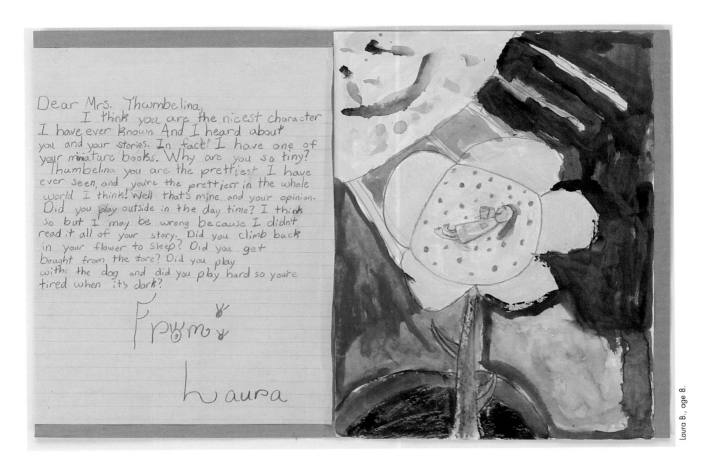

Laura B., age 8.

Adam B., age 5.

Winter Bazaar, third grade project, Sherman Elementary. Audry Grandi, teacher.

Chapter Five

Ideas, Environment, and Guidance

Photo by Barbara McGuire.

Providing Environment and Direction

As much as it is necessary to encourage innovation and creativity in a child, there is also a need to establish a structure that facilitates creativity. Structure will nurture children's beliefs that they are in a safe environment where they can create without harm or damage to themselves or property.

It is not advised to simply let a child loose and see what happens. Children require direction not only for their personal safety, but also for the preservation of property. Direction is also useful in *teaching* the child how to be creative without harming others or property.

A good way to start any project is to start with a clean workspace and a clean child—peas and carrots are not meant to be painting media. Wash your child's hands before you begin to create. See that the child's clothing is protected. Provide adequate light. Position the child so that she can move freely. Position the child so that he will not accidentally draw on tables or walls. Teach the child that pencils and crayons and paints belong on paper—are not to be eaten—and that they belong in special places within the household.

With unlimited possibilities at hand, it is reasonable that the child be directed so that choices are not so overwhelming. Children thrive on consistency. They thrive on structure. It is healthy to discover, explore, be creative, and be unique. It is through learning that we are able to follow direction. It is through practice that we have faith in direction and the security of the outcome of following direction. It is not healthy to disobey, ignore, and rebel against good advice.

These are principles that you can instill in a child through experiences with art. Choosing color is not controlling a situation—it is limiting choices. Choosing media is not controlling—it is providing direction. The beauty of child art is that the energy and creative spirit still remain free within the choices adults make because child art does not depend on these choices.

When you are with your child, create a comfortable environment for yourself, too. Dress appropriately. Play delightful music. Open the windows. Relax. Focus your attention. Do not try to read a magazine, or watch a video or television. Do not allow the phone to distract you. *Be* with the child. After the child has experienced the security and support of your attention and presence, you can venture to introduce independence during the activity. The child learns to create on his own after he has experienced your guided support and is confident in the environment. Groups of children drawing together are great support. You will notice very young children have little interest in what others are drawing, whereas older children seek to compare works.

After you have provided a creative period with your child, be aware of the manner in which you finish the session. Do you become impatient for the child to finish? Are the materials neatly stowed away? Is the work signed and dated? Is the child's experience reinforced with your praise, acknowledgment, and support? Is the child able to see the art again? Can he show it to his friends and family? Do you throw the art away? All these things subtly direct the outcome of the experience, and either nurture or tear down the creative spirit.

Dori K, Sherman Elementary kindergarten. Youth Arts Festival, 2001.

Rachelle L., age 7, Clear Creek Elementary School, Sakura's Wonderful, Colorful World Contest. Wendy Ping, teacher.

Kayla V., age 8, Clear Creek Elementary School, Sakura's Wonderful, Colorful World Contest. Wendy Ping, teacher.

Teaching Skills—Teaching Results

All adults are teachers in a child's world—remember, "It takes a village." That is because the children absorb the habits of adults. But the child is still a child who needs to understand what *directions* are, or what *goals* are. You must teach a child that a crayon makes a mark on a piece of paper; she cannot make this connection independently of you. Children learn by example. You can't expect the child to know what you want, nor does the child learn by simply seeing a piece that is already complete. The child must see the action that produces the result. We forget to show the child how to create. So, go ahead and scribble; show the child how to create.

One view, one experience, is not adequate to fill the child with enough information to achieve control. It takes practice. It takes seeing things over and over. Practice produces a familiarity that feeds the confidence to go on to the next step, to experiment and experience further. You shortchange a child when you only give him one try, one possibility to achieve something. How many attempts does it take to learn to talk, or to walk? What if you were only given one attempt to shoot a basketball in a hoop? Even the person with the most potential could be discouraged to the point of quitting, if not given enough chances.

We have to state our expectations, and illustrate how and why these expectations can be achieved. For example, if you are making a bug and the child is directed to make little pieces, those little pieces at first will be really wacky. These little, wacky pieces give you an opportunity to encourage the child to get the pieces smoother, rounder, with more attention to form and size. If you are trying to explain how to draw a straight line, or color in the lines, show the child how to do it. Do not merely explain in words

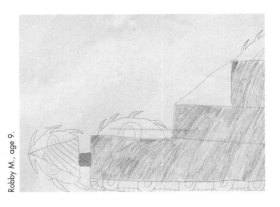

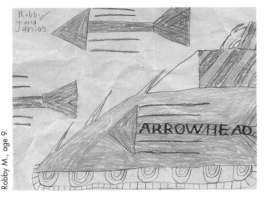

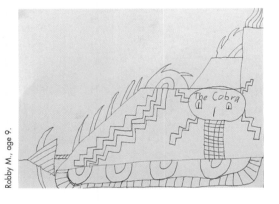

and assume the child can translate words into physical direction. Sometimes it is also helpful to have a finished example so the child can see it, *and* the steps that were needed to achieve that result.

Practice. There is no substitute for practice. Allow for projects to be done more than once. This is really important. Children need a second try so they can continue experiencing, creating, improving. I learned this during a Christmas project with a group of twenty third graders. We were making little dolls out of polymer clay, and I had only brought enough supplies and furnished enough time to make one doll per person. Not only were the children disappointed that they could not make another, but it was evident that they had just begun to catch on to the concept of the doll, and had used up the learning experience to make the first doll; but now they were ready to create! Their regular teacher actually continued the program, but I learned that the potential escalates with each endeavor.

Teach children to make several pictures. We are trained to constantly correct and modify our initial attempt, to the point that it is worked and reworked. Instead, complete several projects and improve with each attempt. If we teach our children to accept and learn from the attempts in which we have little experience, little practice, and little knowledge, we can show them the outcome of training. If we strive to hide inexperience, cover up mistakes, disrespect the learning process, we are in fact expecting accomplished results without practice. What you do in their young years will affect them now, and will help them to develop patience and encouragement for when they are learning to master other skills, such as printing and writing words.

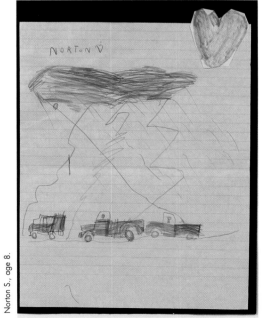

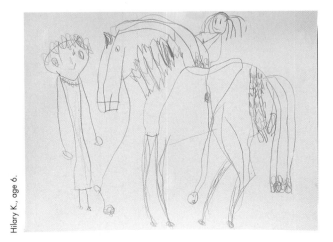

It is a sheer joy to view the transition among levels of development revealed in a first set of scribbles and the later drawings of a child. Keep the drawings for comparison and for discussion about colors, size, direction of line, inclusion of objects. Talk to your children about the drawings, but do not ask for justification or imply disappointment: "Why did you ____?" or, "Don't you think ____?" Don't falsely praise. Simply make observational statements, such as "I see that this line goes up," or "That looks like a circle." Let the child fill in the story and voice his art in relation to his thoughts. You will find that children have very definite ideas about their own art, its need for addition or its state of completion. You will discover at what point the child has grasped what is to be learned from the creative experience. And she will be satisfied with her experience.

Chance O., age 7, "5580 John Deere." Rheata White Studio, Sakura's Wonderful, Colorful World Contest. Rheata White, teacher.

Molly S., age 7, "My Own Creation." Grace Episcopal Day School, Sakura's Wonderful, Colorful World Contest. Kris Lesak, teacher.

Julian C., age 9.

Chloe A., age 10.

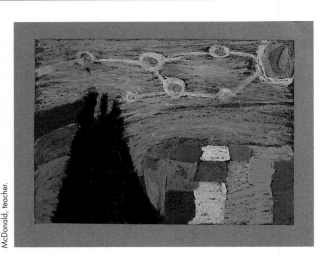

Alexander J., age 7, "Starry Sky." State Bridge Crossing School, Sakura's Wonderful, Colorful World Contest. Marilyn Katz, teacher.

Tylor R., age 8, "Just Like VanGogh." C.P. Squires Elementary School, Sakura's Wonderful, Colorful World Contest. Cindy McDonald, teacher.

Jessica S., age 7, " Just Like Picasso." C.P. Squires Elementary School, Sakura's Wonderful, Colorful World Contest. Cindy McDonald, teacher.

Trey D., age 7, Our Lady of Perpetual Help School, Sakura's Wonderful, Colorful World Contest. Ann Meinert, teacher.

Jenna L., age 7, Herman Elementary School, Sakura's Wonderful, Colorful World Contest. Rachel Case, teacher.

Joshua Y., age 7, Herman Elementary School, Sakura's Wonderful, Colorful World Contest. Rachel Case, teacher.

Matthew N., age 8, Herman Elementary School, Sakura's Wonderful, Colorful World Contest. Rachel Case, teacher.

Hayley T., age 7, Herman Elementary School, Sakura's Wonderful, Colorful World Contest. Rachel Case, teacher.

The thinking of young children is qualitatively different from that of adults. They are constantly operating within the process of constructing their knowledge. They are learning about the physical world, how it works and the relationships between these operations.

Each time children have an opportunity to represent and discuss the world that they are experiencing, there is an opportunity to build complexity in the organizational structures of their thinking. Because of this complexity, children have formed multiple strategies and points of reference to access and use from which to infer meaning while reading or navigating through life.

Art is taken very seriously as one of the keys to the child's discovery process. Many media for representation are offered to the children as they discover and build theories about the physical world around them. Each medium has different qualities to offer, initiating a unique discovery.

Though not often thought of as an art form for young children, photography gives us a view of what the child has observed. Through discussion and listening to the child tell and re-tell their responses to an item in their photograph, we gain insight into the child's thinking. We become better acquainted with the context of the child's world. In essence, we become better listeners.

For the children, photography can be a powerful tool to revisit experiences. Where drawing involves the sensorimotor responses to an item, photography is more similar to capturing the essence of an item, similar to a piece of evidence. In this sense, the distance from the immediacy of the moment affords the child time to review and reflect. In other words, the child has the luxury of time to savor the moment.

-Elizabeth Heffernan, while working on her master's thesis in child development.

Choosing Materials

One of the most important things to stress is that we get better results with sophisticated materials. Investing in good materials is minimal and paramount to the art. Many art programs are funded by teachers without budgets, so it's no wonder that good materials are scarce. And, to make matters worse, most companies make things for kids to produce art that is meant to be expendable. I was never versed in the temporary life of a crayon. I always thought construction paper kept its color. Some of the work seems to dissolve before my very eyes. I've seen more hair come out of a kid's paintbrush than our cat. Manufacturers have different "grades" of pencils, papers, chalks, and clays. For a child, there is no difference in "practice" and the "real" thing. Children don't say to themselves, "Okay, I have practiced and now I am going to make a better piece of work, so I need to switch to my 'good' materials." All child art is the real thing. At this stage there is no concept of practice. Each piece is exactly what it needs to be to experience the process.

Like every mom on a budget, I have cringed when I see my children "waste" a piece of fine Bristol or watercolor paper. But if I would only compare how many times I have taken and developed a whole roll of film just to get one good shot, my attitude becomes much more generous. I also remember experiencing remorse when a really good piece of art is drawn on the backside of an outdated notice. There is no comparison to what parents spend on videos, action figures, fashion dolls, and plastic play sets. Why, why, why won't we invest in art?

I have spent more on wooden trains than I will spend on art materials in three years. All of childhood is learning, and children need to learn from art as much as they need to learn from trains or dolls.

Photo by Jay Jones. Madison and McKenzie L. discovering Duva Heat-set Pastels.

Photo by Riley H., age 7.

I think that when we're young, creativity is easy. All we need is something to create on——a sidewalk, a wall, a piece of paper, and something to create with——crayons, chalk, mud! We can do it for fun and the pleasure of showing off——"Look what I made!" I certainly remember making things, especially drawings, all the time when I was a child. And early on I developed a real taste for the "good stuff"——clean, unwrinkled paper, not the backs of old letters and brochures, and new markers instead of broken crayons or dull pencils.

Now that I am a parent, I see the same inclination in my kids and their friends. I've noticed, too, that they seem to give their best efforts when they have the "good stuff." They take a little more time and pay more attention to details. They are a little more proud when they show it to me. The best of their best goes on display: "Look what I made."

-Christi, a parent

Celina L., age 7, "Ocean Life," Pinewood Elementary School, Sakura's Wonderful, Colorful World Contest. Kathleen Winters, teacher.

When I discovered that it was okay to give children good stuff, I started to do some experiments with my kids, giving them different materials. Their work improved dramatically when I gave them good paper. I think of the importance of paper in our society, of how much I like to read a book printed on good paper. I think of the impact card stock has over a flimsy brochure. I don't doubt that children notice these things, too.

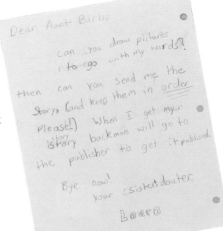

Laura B., age 7.

In the great paper chase we need to stop and give our kids a piece of decent paper. They can handle the good paper and pens. Today's fine-line ink pens are incredible tools to give to children. The tips are tough, and they can handle them just as easily as the tips of crayons. The metallics are incredible. Who could ever dream of a shimmering gold line across a jet-black space? Children can. We have achieved an incredible technical leap and have not brought it to our developing children. It seems we would rather "wow" them with blinking, talking toys.

Tiffany C., age 7, "Flower Power." Walt Whitman Elementary School, Sakura's Wonderful, Colorful World Contest. Mrs. Levien, teacher.

And Then There Are My Materials

Kids are still kids; they have to be taught. They don't know that you don't dip a paintbrush full of black paint into yellow. They don't know that you need to change the water; they must be taught. They need to learn. That is why you don't give them your materials. Every time I get over-ambitious and want to let the kids use my stuff, I am abashed at their lack of common sense and disregard for organization. Maybe the stretch of forty years has some-

Lilla C., age 6, "Flowers in Vase." American School of Antananarivo, Madagascar. Sakura's Wonderful, Colorful World Contest. Rhoda Jordaan, teacher.

thing to do with it. Kids are still kids—organization doesn't yet make sense to them. In actuality, they don't care if they destroy the yellow watercolor. It is just a losing battle to keep crayons whole, colors in order, paints separated and clay un-smashed—there is no quicker route to frustration than to try doing so.

So you set limits. Their little hands must do something while you prepare yourself for reckless abandon. You don't give them time to mess up the project before you even start. They are going to start immediately, without direction, when you put something in front of them. Give them wire to twirl, give them clay to squish, give them paper to cut. Give them shapes to glue onto paper with a glue stick.

Frustrated parents are not going to tolerate a child discovering art unless they are prepared. So prepare: the table, the clothes, the floor, and your own attire—and grab the art when it's done. Don't let it get altered, spilled on, scribbled on, stepped on, crumpled. You can't even turn around, they are that fast. The experience is completely predictable in that the beauty of the art is completely unpredictable; but the effort is *worth* the investment.

Cherie O., age 7, Tule Elk Park.

Caitlyn P., age 11, "Sublime." St. Mark's Lutheran School, Sakura's Wonderful, Colorful World Contest. Gopika Parikh, teacher.

Chapter Six

Letting Go — and Having Fun

Photo by Barbara McGuire. Maisy and Stan.

Once I was at a school fundraiser doing crafts with the children. There, I noticed a parent who was helping her daughter to make a little pin out of clay. The mother, though well intentioned, kept reaching around the child and saying "Don't you want to choose *this* color? Wouldn't you like to place that *here*?" I invited the parent to make a piece herself but she firmly declined.

This experience was very impacting, and revealed two things to me. First, the mother was more interested in what *she* wanted as opposed to what the *child* wanted, and second, the mother would rather *tell* the child what to do than *show* her what to do.

There are all sorts of adult issues that come to surface when doing art with children. It can be really hard to show restraint. I think that is true in most of life but we take an extra measure of control when it is our own child. Control is good when you are crossing the street, but it is an obstacle when your children are creating art. I found it hard to believe that the little girl I witnessed would be able to stand up for her own decisions. She would need to have a lot of courage to disagree with her mother's choices. Faced with such conflict, it is easy to become frustrated and simply become resentful or give up. With all my adult powers I could not gracefully encourage the mother to allow her daughter to create, and I wondered if the mother would ever trust the child to make a decision.

Another adult issue is getting over the age barrier of teaching and playing art with your child. Some adults will not, or cannot, permit themselves to do something that is not serious and correct. I personally had a very hard time playing dolls with little girls or cars with little boys. I had not used my imagination for play in so long, it was hard to fantasize; I quickly ran out of ideas for dialog between toys and children. The same is possible when drawing with children. We quickly exhaust the typical scenarios of

Eric S., age 5, "Walk on the Wild Side." *Young at Art Children's Museum, Sakura's Wonderful, Colorful World Contest.* Nichelle Notabartolo, teacher.

"flower," "sun," and "person." Our memory banks are not full of childish ideas. We are so proper, so refined, so erased, that there are no beautiful mistakes left for us to celebrate. When your child needs an example to follow, you need to recall the bubbles, the bugs, the presents, the splashes, the giggles, the tickles, and the barnyard creatures that talk. The imagination will come forth once you let it out of jail. Do the art with the child. Have fun yourself.

Teach a child when to stop. Teach the child to be satisfied. Teach the child that much like there is always a new day, there is a new piece of paper. Teach a child that each work is enough in itself. There is no one ultimate piece of art. Just as nature has many flowers, so children create many different works of art. But each one is singularly beautiful.

Accept their results. Don't change the art. This is a lesson I still need to learn, over and over again. The temptation to refine the art is overwhelming. If you want to make a suggestion, be humble enough to ask permission to touch the art. Admittedly, I have seen children cry because I have made a line on their art. It should come as no surprise that they are so attached to their art. It should come as no surprise that they like what they created and they are sensitive to its being altered in any way.

Children will want to create art for their friends. It will be very hard to give up your child's art that *you* wanted. This is another lesson in letting go. Assure yourself that there will always be more. The experience of letting your child give something that they have independently created is crucial in relating to the joy of giving.

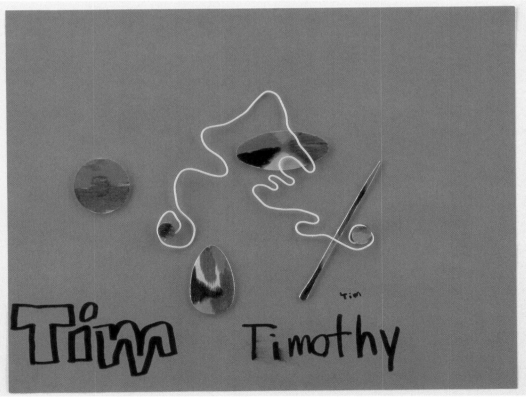

Tim M., Tule Elk Park, San Francisco Youth Art Festival 2000.

Sometimes it can be a shock to see how children are attached to something that you think is of no value. The word "mine" is very relatable to children and their art. *Never* let your children see their work in the garbage. Of course it is impossible to keep all their art, but you can find a way to discuss with your child what is their favorite and be sure to treat that with special respect.

Respect the art. One of the most brazen ways to destroy a piece of child art is to print a name on the front of the work. I am not saying the art should not be signed. Indeed it should—but with appropriateness, on the backside, or in the child's own writing. At certain ages, the child will make the signature a predominant feature of the work. This is something reflective of the child's emerging identity, and the discovered ability to claim that identity. The child does not realize the signature is separate from the art. It is a time for patience and guidance to teach the child how to appropriately sign the art. Again, you cannot take it for granted that this is something the child already knows.

In recent years, pastimes focusing on scrap booking and journaling have grown to a

Sara W. K-12 Gallery for Young People, Dayton, Ohio.

Samson Z., Tule Elk Park, San Francisco Youth Arts Festival 2000.

I have saved artworks from Henri's finger paintings at two years old to his current, seven-year-old objects. Recently, for my own art studies, I took a short workshop in book/shadow-box construction. For the class book, I needed artwork as content, so rather than using my own artworks, I sifted through Henri's artwork. I had to decide what and how I was willing to cut-to-fit into the book format. Ultimately, I altered very little. I did exercise great care and attention to sequencing and placement. Henri loves his book, especially since I made the effort to pull his artwork together as a formal object.

-Deborah Colotti

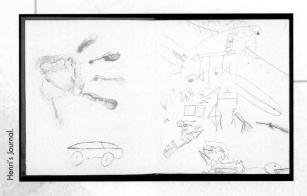

Henri's Journal.

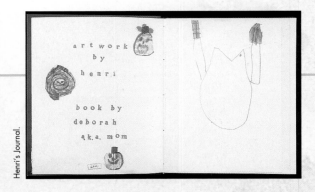

Henri's Journal.

Henri's Journal.

Henri's Journal.

national phenomenon. Some of this is due to the commercial efforts to encourage self-discovery and expression through documentation. Another influence has been the activity of creating journals throughout the schools across the nation in the primary years. I must admit that of all the papers brought home from school, the journals are the ones I keep. They are the most precious documentation of a developing mind. The art and the stories play off each other to showcase a child's simple, straightforward view of life. But this is not without complication or detail. Pictures reveal highlights and recognition in a child's environment.

Tim M., age 6.

The words that accompany a picture further enforce the child's intention of communication. Words at a later time will be capable of describing imaginings that are not real, or ideas that cannot be realized through pictures. Allowing a child to be expressive in pictures lays a foundation for the imagination to be creative with words.

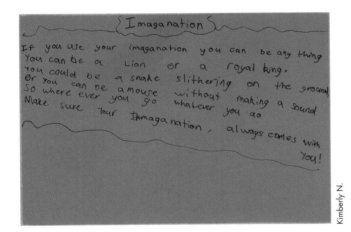

Kimberly N.

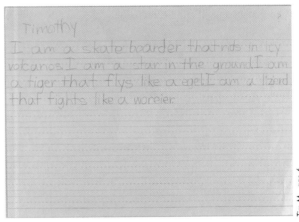

Tim M., age 6.

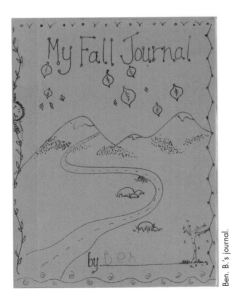

Ben. B.'s journal.

Ben. B.'s journal.

Ben. B.'s journal.

"Three men built this house. In this house, they planted the trees for the bugs to live. They made a laboratory to drink water, cafeteria to eat. They planted the flowers so that they can smell whenever they wanted. One of the garden builders built a TV so he can watch and to see how it works. One man is hammering a nail and two men came to help. One of the bugs they put in the garden is butterfly. It is crawling on the house. The bugs will live here forever and ever, happily. After they built the house, builders invited more bugs—there will be millions of them living there."

-Kevin L., age 5, describing his ink drawing (below).

Kevin L., Tule Elk Park, Yuko Marshall, teacher.

Letting Go — and Having Fun

Chapter Seven

Materials and Projects

Photo by Barbara McGuire Annette Litle and Tynani.

The Projects in This Book

Note: Projects are for adults to do with children's art. Please note labeling on products; individual choices of materials such as varnishes, carving tools, and permanent inks may not be suitable for children.

These projects cannot be done without a child. But they are not for children to manage. You do not have to be an artist to do the projects; they can be done by anyone who does not have experience in using art materials. The projects just *look* artistic. They are really very easy. Basic skills such as tracing, cutting, painting, and coloring are required, but most of us have enough skills if we have managed to raise a child.

The projects present creative ways to bring your children's art into everyday life. They are very personal to the family; no one walking through the door is going to notice that Timmy's snowflake design is the pattern on the table runner. It's that special, subtle secret that you can boast about over dinner. No one is going to know that your child's first drawings are pasted in your journal. But you will see them every time you write, and *you* will know.

Photo by Jay Jones. Tim M.

Since there are a lot of different types of projects, I have presented the materials as each project appears. There is usually more than one option for materials to complete a project. There may only be one brand of paper, paint, glue, or scissors available at your store. Many of the materials can be substituted with whatever products are available to you. Since you are always working with children's art, none of the projects will ever look exactly like the sample. But they will be exactly what they are supposed to be and they will be special.

The projects are for all ages. You will get different results using art from children of different ages, but it will all be appealing. Once you have familiarized yourself with the materials, you might consider doing other projects with the same materials.

There are also a few "pointers" in general about materials: For example, an explanation about the difference between hot- and cold-press watercolor paper is just for information. The more information you have about something, the less you fear new experiences. Information provides options. In the source listing of the book, there are manufacturers listed that are able to answer specific questions. But the best way to gain knowledge is to share it. After you have success with a project in your home, go to your school, or church, or scout group, or recreation center and offer to participate in an art project. Not only will you further your education, but you will be encouraging a young, creative spirit.

Project 1

Mini Masterpiece Journal

When I asked one of my friends for her child's early drawings she hesitated, saying "I'm not sure you can tell what they are." "It doesn't matter," I replied. "They're still cool. I can take some part of them, and do something that will be really special." I began to experiment with the drawing in miniature. The original drawings, reduced nearly to one-tenth the original size, were very appealing. Then, I was able to apply them in a way that was intensely personal: a journal, just for mom. It doesn't matter if it means anything to anyone else. The project actually became a good way to make a great instant gift for relatives or friends of any age.

There were many options as how to secure the drawing on the journal. As I experimented, I learned about the differences in finishes. Use a dry double-stick glue (or very light coats of collage gel or Perfect Paper Adhesive) to adhere the print to the journal because you don't want the print to absorb the finish and change color. Because you will be using a computer, and the original is still intact, you can try over and over again until you get the desired effect.

Hint: When paper gets wet, it wrinkles. Keep this to a minimum with thin coats of adhesive. Try to "seal" drawings by using consistent coverage. There will be no "glue" spots.

Jonathan E.

Photo by Barbara McGuire. Brenda Johnson and Bryant.

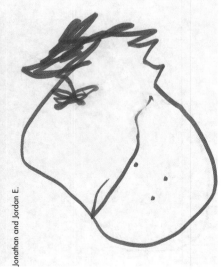

Jonathan and Jordan E.

Instructions

1. Scale the drawing/painting to size and reproduce on heavy quality paper or card stock. The paper should have a high brightness and be a heavy stock. Many times I will use quality brochure paper or paper especially for photo computer reprinting. Most color copiers in a copy service place will provide adequate paper, but you can always ask them to print on your paper.

2. Trim the reduced print with a paper cutter. The clean cut of a paper cutter will make all the difference in the world when it comes to a straight edge. Many copy centers also have cutters available. You can trim just outside the print's edge for a decorative border if desired.

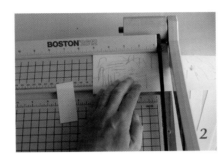

3. Attach the paper to the dry adhesive. Dry adhesive is actually glue that is sandwiched between two layers of release paper. First cut the dry adhesive to an approximate size of the print. Peel off one side of the release paper and smooth the reprint on the tacky surface. Burnish the print to the glue with a bone burnisher (this is an incredible tool that smoothes out air bubbles and encourages a tight seal). You can also use the back of a spoon. Trim the adhesive to fit the exact size of the print. Be careful—the adhesive is very strong. Do not allow it to fall on carpet or on your clothes; it will be difficult to remove.

4. With the journal close at hand, remove the remaining release paper and place the print on the journal. Begin at one end and position evenly and smooth to the other end. You may not get a chance to reposition. The glue is very sticky. Sometimes I only begin to expose the glue and gently place the piece so I can reposition the print. You don't want it crooked on the journal.

5. After the print is positioned and secured, burnish the print so it really sticks and eliminates air pockets. Don't scratch the print. Use the bone burnisher or the back of a spoon.

6. Next protect the finish with a layer of art sealer.

7. Add multiple layers of sealant, Mod Podge, or Perfect Paper Adhesive to finish and protect the art.

Materials

- Paper journal
- Drawing from children (resized)
- Computer color photocopy on card stock paper
- Graphix dry adhesive, scissors
- Bone burnisher
- Soft brush for sealant
- Crafter's Pick Art sealant
- Collage finish such as Perfect Paper Adhesive, or Mod Podge
- Paper cutter

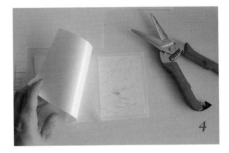

Folk Animal Felts

Very young children delight in this project because it is so straightforward. It is a wonderfully interactive project in which the adult can cut the pieces and the child can place them. The way children place shapes is extremely charming and the simplicity is reflective of folk art. Their sense of representation is based on a priority of parts rather than realism. Minute details such as tails, whiskers, and ears are priorities to the child.

It helps if they have an example to follow and a story to describe. Often the animals are pictured with babies, a smaller version of the original animal. The choice of colors and materials will dictate the mood of the piece; if the felt and fabric reflect earthy, muted colors, the piece will look more "country." Using pinking shears to cut some of the pieces adds a nice touch although the material must be finely woven to prevent unraveling. This is a nice project to frame or position on a hanging banner.

Photo by Barbara McGuire. Janelle A.

Janelle, Age 4, Tule Elk Park, Yuko Marshall, teacher.

Vivian, age 4, Tule Elk Park, Yuko Marshall, teacher.

Maisy, Age 4, Tule Elk Park, Yuko Marshall, teacher.

Scarlet, age 4, Tule Elk Park, Yuko Marshall, teacher.

Instructions

1. Cut shapes for the animal. A box for the body, a rectangle for the head and four sticks for the legs. Cut a tail, ears and other details as the child suggests. The child will be able to cut the shapes if the material is stiff enough, but in many cases, children's scissors will only pinch the fabric.

2. Ask the child to build the animal on the quilt as you cut the shapes.

3. When the composition is placed, begin to glue the pieces.

4. Remove the body and, using the craft stick, evenly spread the entire back with a light coat of glue.

5. Have the child replace the body.

6. Glue each piece, one at a time, handing the glued piece back to the child to be replaced in the composition.

Materials

- 8" x 11" felt in a muted color (heather colors)
- Assorted complementary felt colors
- Scraps of fabric in classic weaves, muted colors
- Scissors
- Optional pinking shears (use on tightly woven fabric or felt)
- Stitchless fabric glue
- Wooden craft stick or brush for spreading glue

Precious Bracelet

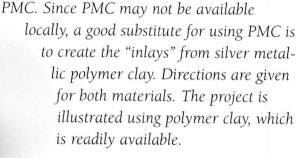

This bracelet is a great example of how to use children's art to make a classy and memorable piece. The secret is tiny, little pieces of PMC, Precious Metal Clay, embedded into polymer clay. PMC is silver metal "clay" in pliable form which, once fired, turns into 99-percent pure silver. Note: the child only pushes the wire into the silver; the child does not handle PMC. Since PMC may not be available locally, a good substitute for using PMC is to create the "inlays" from silver metallic polymer clay. Directions are given for both materials. The project is illustrated using polymer clay, which is readily available.

Materials

- Precious Metal Clay or silver metallic polymer clay (Premo)
- Acrylic brayer or clay roller (you can also use a straight glass)
- 1 block of translucent Polymer clay (Premo), bits of green clay (1/4" diameter), and a tiny bit of orange clay (a crumb)—mixed to make a "jade green" color
- 2' telephone wire, 22 gauge, cut into six 4" lengths
- Paper strip 1" x 10", tape
- Oven for baking clay, kiln for firing PMC (or send away to have fired)
- Card stock paper for work and baking surface
- Polymer clay blade
- Burnt sienna acrylic paint, application brush
- 600 grit wet sand paper

Instructions

1. Make spirals and swigglies in the wires at the very end of the wire. Bend the remaining length upward to create a "handle." The resulting tool will look like a miniature "branding iron." (Depending on the dexterity of the child, they may actually be able to do this step.) Set aside.

2. Roll the PMC or silver polymer clay into a strip 1/2" x 4" long and 1/16" thick. Note: PMC will dry quickly, especially in small amounts, so be prepared to roll a strip and imprint it immediately. Polymer clay must be conditioned before use. That is, it must be made pliable by kneading.

3. Using the shaped wires, ask your child to "brand" or imprint the strip with random design.

4. Once imprinted, cut the strip into little blocks of design and cure. PMC must first be allowed to air dry and then made permanent by professionally firing in a kiln (see drying instructions from the supplier of the Precious Metal Clay. Polymer clay can be baked in an oven as the manufacturer directs (usually 275° F. for 20 minutes).

5. Mix the translucent, green, and orange polymer clay to condition the clay and create a jade green color. Note: Substitute your own color for personal preference. These steps illustrate using gold Premo.

6. Roll a strip of clay 1" wide, 8" long, and approximately 3/16" thick. My favorite method for rolling a strip is to make a snake and then flatten it with the brayer. That way the edges are rounded.

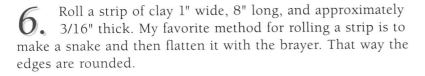

7. Wrap the paper strip around your wrist and tape it at a comfortable length. The bracelet will have an opening, but measure to approximate the desired size.

8. Arrange the little blocks of imprinted (cured) silver or silver polymer clay on top of the strip.

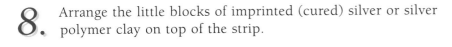

9. Press gently to embed the pieces into the strip. Push the strip closer together and in at the top and bottom to "overlap" the design pieces slightly.

10. Gently pick up the piece from the work area and wrap around the paper band in an oval shape. Trim the clay strip so the ends are facing each other with approximately 1" gap. This is where the bracelet will slip on and off the wrist once it is baked.

11. Bake the piece as the manufacturer directs.

12. When the bracelet is cool, paint it with burnt sienna acrylic paint. Be sure to get in all the little cracks, including those between the silver and green clays, as well as the wire impressions.

13. After the paint is dry, sand the bracelet with 600 grit wet sand paper to remove the paint from the surface, but not the grooves, of the bracelet. The bracelet may also be buffed for an additional shine.

Jason's Ladder

Project 4

This project took Jason Ghiraduzzi and his dad about five minutes to paint and me about two hours to compose. I was very picky about the combination of materials. It had to be just right to do justice to the drawing/painting. But there is something about someone else's art (even your own child's, or a friend's child) that is incredibly freeing. Not only do you want to take care to complete a project with a nice finish but also you are more willing to experiment. This project started out with scribbles and ended up being one of the most elegant projects in the collection. The composition is built on repetition and balance. It is also an opportunity to use elegant ribbon, sheer fabric, and pretty, handmade papers. The fun part is to pick out highlights of the original watercolor and then place it back together like an abstract puzzle.

Photo by Jay Jones. Jason and David.

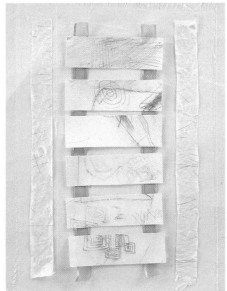

Materials

- Watercolor paper, cold-press*
- Water-soluble colored pencil
- Pen, scissors
- Water, brush
- 1" sheer, wide ribbon with satin edges
- 2 handmade pieces of paper (one for background, and one for highlights)
- Fabric glue
- Spray adhesive
- Gauze-type fabric
- Old newsprint

*Note: Cold-press paper has a texture or tooth; hot-press paper has a smooth texture.

Instructions

1. Make a pencil drawing with your child, allowing him to scribble, overlapping the drawings. If you are short of drawing ideas, use spirals, labyrinths, nested circles, etc. Leave some space between drawn objects.

2. Dampen the brush with water and paint the paper. This will smear and blend some of the colors. Use the water sparingly and adjust the wetness by blotting the brush if necessary.

3. Thank your child for his help. Allow the work to dry.

4. Choose a rectangle shape and cut a pattern out of plastic, tracing paper, or some-

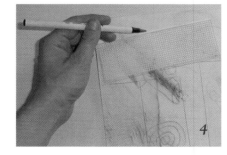

thing you can see through. Pick out interesting points in the drawing and outline the rectangle in pen. Cut the rectangles.

5. Line up the rectangles, keeping 1" between each drawing and turn them over, face down.

6. Place fabric glue about 1-1/2" from the edge down the strip of rectangles.

7. Glue a wide ribbon vertically connecting the rectangles.

8. Cut a piece of gauze large enough to accommodate 4" on all sides of the ladder. Take note of the weave of the gauze and place the ladder parallel to the weave. Glue the "ladder" to the gauze with fabric glue.

9. Trim the gauze if necessary and fray the edges.

10. Spread newsprint to create a surface for spraying the adhesive. Turn the piece over and spray with spray adhesive.

11. Glue the gauze and ladder on a piece of old, handmade paper.

12. Cut two strips of another handmade paper. The one showing has strips of gold metallic thread through it.

13. Coat the back of these strips with spray adhesive. Place the strips on either side of the ladder.

14. Frame or hang as a poster-type piece of art.

8

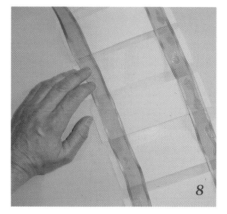

8

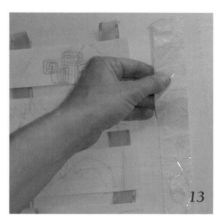

13

Table Runner

Sooner or later, every child will bring home a snowflake that is the envy of Jack Frost. These folded bits of clipped paper are fascinating. The rectangular "snowflake" you see here is the pattern used in the classic table runner. Using the table runner everyday reminds me of when my son first came home with his collection and his amazement of the secrets of mirror imaging.

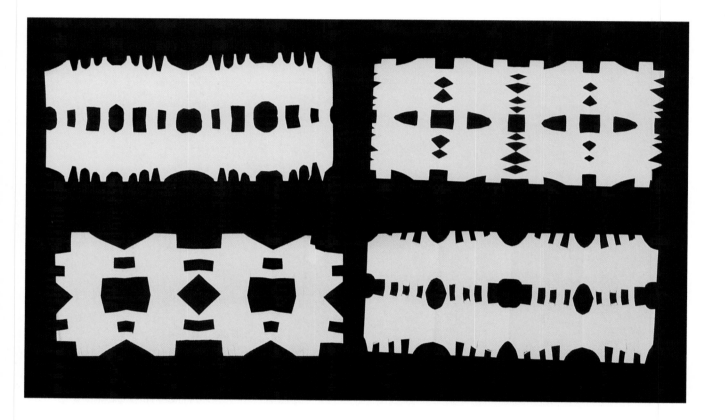

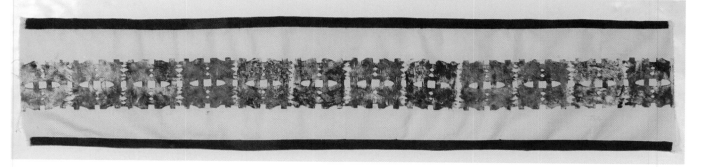

Instructions

1. Fold the paper in half lengthwise and then again to make four vertical folds. Fold the paper across the folds, horizontally.

2. Cut the edges of the folded paper with little triangles, half circles, and odd shapes. Make several.

3. Open the paper and look at it. Decide which pattern you like the best. You will only need to use half of the paper because the design repeats itself. Using a fine tip marker, outline half of the design on a square of craft foam.

4. Place the foam on a piece of scrap cardboard. Carefully cut the design from the foam using an X-Acto craft knife.

5. Spread the paint on a plastic surface (or heavy paper, cardboard, etc.). Mix two colors to get streaks in the paint. Wet the foam. This helps to release the paint on the fabric.

6. Spread the paint onto the foam with the roller.

7. Fold the cloth in half lengthwise and, beginning in the center aligned on one side of the fold, stamp the painted foam on the fabric.

8. Place the next design aligned to the first imprint and continue to paint the foam and stamp the fabric.

9. When the paint gets too tacky and will not print, wash the foam and start over. Repeat stamping if you wish to add more color, or if the original stamp did not imprint as desired.

10. Allow the paint to dry completely. Depending on the type of fabric paint used, you may have to heat-set it to make it permanent. Create fringe on the edges of the runner by pulling the threads through the material.

Tip: Save the stamp to decorate and use as the background to a rubber stamp collage.

Materials

- Rectangle of white paper (5" x 11"), several for different designs
- Scissors
- Heavy muslin cloth 5' x 14" (tight weave)
- Fabric paint, navy and iridescent gold
- Scrap cardboard
- Sheet of craft foam
- Rubber roller for paint
- X-Acto knife
- Fine-tip marker

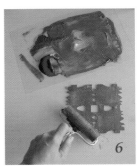

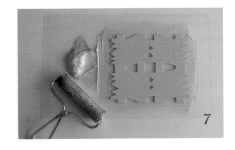

Stamped Stationery

Rubber stamps are a great way to share a special design with all your pen pals. It is very easy to create your own stamps. Companies like Staedtler Mars and Speedball have produced a rubber medium that is great for transferring drawing and carving with a nib. The rubber is capable of erasing pencil and film but, once carved, it can be inked and used as a stamp. The inks currently on the market are incredible and colorful. They can be used to decorate paper and cloth easily. Another tip about making stamps is that you can section out several small characters in a drawing, and then make a story with the stamps using the characters independently.

Photo by Barbara McGuire. Kevin L.

Instructions

1. Trace the child's image into tracing paper. Note that the image will be reversed (a mirror image). If you want an exact transfer, you can flip the tracing paper and trace the lines again.

2. Transfer the drawing to the rubber by burnishing with a bone burnisher or rubbing with the back of a spoon. The pencil will transfer to the rubber.

3. Carve the lines with the thinnest nib carver. Turn the work to guide the carved lines so you have a steady carve and can position your hand to comfortably reach all the work.

4. Test sample the inks and paper to see which combination you prefer. (See Special note on inks and papers on page 135.)

5. Stamp the rubber on the pad and then stamp the paper.

6. For cards, cut a shape from the stamped paper, square, or otherwise, and place it on the card. You can also stamp on vellum and layer the papers for an interesting effect, but you must heat set the ink with a heat gun.

Materials

- Child's line drawing*
- Tracing paper, pencil
- Bone burnisher or spoon
- Staedtler Mars plastic or Speedball rubber stamp block
- Tiny nib linoleum carver in handle (Speedball)
- Permanent Ink in pad (Memories)
- Paper stationery
- Special papers
- Blank cards

*Note: You can use any line drawing. If it is pencil, it will transfer directly to the rubber. If it is marker, use tracing paper and trace with a pencil. If it is too large for the project, scale it to the desired size to fit the stamp.

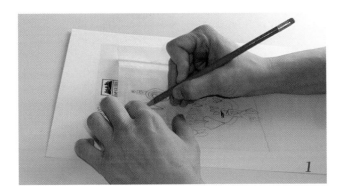

Carved Plate

Here's a simple project, with amazing results. Not only will your child's drawing be properly "framed," it's likely this piece will last many years.

You can ask your child to help roll out the clay—but be sure to wash hands afterwards.

Instructions

1. Have your child draw or trace a design onto tracing paper. You can use a computer, or copier to scan and rescale the drawing to any size you wish, but the final drawing should accommodate a 1/2" border. Cut the drawing to a size that you will use as a template.

2. Photocopy the drawing. When you place it on the clay, it will produce a mirror-image.

3. Condition the clay. Roll the gold clay into a large, flat sheet, about 1/8"–enough to accommodate the size of the drawing including the border. Trim the clay to the approximate size of the plate.

4. Place the photocopy on the clay and allow it to sit until it transfers to the clay.

5. Remove the paper, revealing the design.

6. With a round embossing tool, trace over the transferred lines. Bear down with enough pressure to "carve" the lines.

7. You may get little "curlies" of clay scrap—that's okay, they also can be picked off after baking. Occasionally pick up the piece and turn it so you can trace well. Pull the stylus toward you with even pressure. Have the child sign or initial the piece while the clay is unbaked.

8. Choose a pre-made cane that will complement your design, or make a jelly roll cane out of two colors (contrasting in value). Jelly roll canes are made by stacking two sheets of clay and rolling into a cylinder. Reduce the cane thickness to 1/4" diameter and slice into thin disks. Decorate the border of the plate with these disks by pressing them onto the surface gently (only to secure them).

9. When you have finished decorating the plate, pull the edges upward (or downward) to give the edges a little flare. Roll a snake and split it half lengthwise. Place two lengths of the half cylinder parallel on the back of the plate.

10. Bake the plate for 20-25 minutes at 265° F. Allow the plate to cool completely. Use as a decoration; the plate is not to be eaten from.

Materials

- Premo, 3 blocks: gold, silver, black
- Toner-based photocopy of drawing
- Ball-point pen or embossing tool
- Child's drawing (to scale)
- Tracing paper
- Opaque paint marker; metallic paint markers
- Pre-made canes, or jelly roll cane
- Roller
- Work surface
- Polymer clay blade
- Pasta machine, if available
- Oven
- Liquitex Burnt Sienna Acrylic

Transferred Lamp

This project is an excellent way to encourage your children and to brighten a room at the same time. You can also make this an interchangeable project to complement any décor. If the drawing is clean, it can be wrapped directly around a small lamp. If it needs to be transferred to a new sheet of paper or screen mesh, you can use any portion of the drawing and place it dramatically in position on the lamp. Keep your eyes open for lamps that will accommodate this type of project. The walls of the lamp need to be straight and sheer, preferably white.

Materials

- Drawing markers
- Double-stick tape or adhesive
- Purchased lamp
- Pencil
- Large sheer, white paper or Japanese screen material

Instructions

1. Choose a very graphic drawing of your child's art. This means a drawing that has bold, clear lines. It can also be colored shapes, but choose something that you can trace and duplicate. Sometimes a small portion of a large drawing is appropriate. You can repeat the same drawing over and over if you wish; for instance, a flower design that has been turned and spaced on the new paper.

2. Purchase a lamp, and white, sheer paper or plastic shade with a flat vertical surface. The lamps I have used are not expensive, ranging from $3 to $25.

3. This paper is Japanese screen material. You can also use a roll of contact paper, but it needs to be sheer enough to trace through. You can also use fabric if you prefer. That may give the lamp a more expensive look. (If you use fabric, you can use a double stick-adhesive such as Graphix that will cover large areas to secure the fabric to the shade.)

4. Select your colored markers and make a test strip on a scrap of paper or fabric to test how the colors will perform on the material. Some colors may bleed into the paper or fabric. Some markers will not give even coverage. I used Identipens by Sakura. Test the glue you plan to use to secure the paper. You want to see if it will buckle the paper, or turn yellow after drying. You can use products like Crafter's Pick or Perfect Paper Adhesive.

5. Measure the circumference and height of the lampshade and add 1-1/2" at the top and bottom. Add 1" to the circumference.

6. Prepare a paper or fabric cover that is the same dimension as the lamp.

7. Trace the child's drawing on the screen material. If the paper is not sheer enough to see through, you can try tracing by placing the pieces on a window to illuminate the drawing and trace it with a pencil. Place the drawing flat on a table and first outline the drawing with the markers, then color it in the same manner as your child to fill in the shapes.

8. Crease the edge of one side of the picture 1" back to make a finished seam. Wrap the transferred art around the lamp, positioning it in place equally over the top and bottom frame. Secure with double-sided tape or glue (remember to complete a glue test in advance). Fold the top and bottom edge over the frame structure of the lamp. Secure with glue or adhesive at spaced intervals, tacking the piece in place.

Turn the shade to an appealing position and enjoy the lamp in your home!

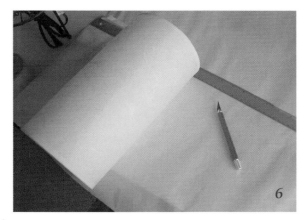

6

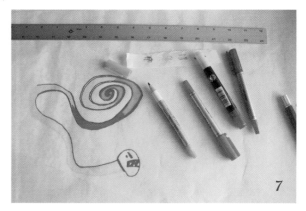

7

Decoupage Chair

I painted this chair white two months ago and found myself staring at it, wondering about stripes and dots. Since I was never a "graphic" person, those types of combinations really challenged me, and I wanted to come up with an alternative. Finally the alternative arrived (in art, sometimes you have to be patient). My inspiration came from furniture I saw in a school auction fundraiser for the Rooftop K-8 Alternative Elementary School in San Francisco.

I came home and leafed through drawings my son had done nearly five years earlier—drawings of knights and castles and swords, things I would never think of as particularly charming. But when the colorful drawings were appliquéd to the white chair, I was astonished at the memories that began to emerge. My son has outgrown the chair, but I don't think I can ever part with it.

Instructions

1. Paint the chair or any article of furniture white. Allow to completely dry.

2. Cut the characters and scenes from an assortment of drawings. Use broad outlined cuts, avoiding a lot of small, thin, protruding pieces.

3. Place a pool of glue on a card stock or cardboard piece, or anything you can brush and blot the glue so there is not too much glue on the brush at any time. Use a thin layer of glue. This is so the paper does not get too wet. Use a piece of scrap paper as a base, and place the cutout face down on the scrap paper. Spread the glue on the back of the drawing with a wide brush. The brush glides the glue off the edge of the cut drawing onto the scrap paper. The scrap paper has to be changed frequently, but the glue goes all the way to the edge with this method, which is also used in making books.

4. Place the cut drawing on the chair. Gently smooth the paper if it wrinkles or has air bubbles. Be careful not to rip it.

5. Continue to glue drawings to the chair as directed above. Place drawings on top of each other if desired.

6. Place cut drawings around the legs too. Be sure to cut out the child's signature if a name is on the drawing and place it somewhere on the chair. You want your chair to be a "signed piece."

7. Allow the glued paper to dry.

8. Spray the chair with Crystal Clear varnish. Allow the varnish to dry between coats.

Materials

- Set of drawings, preferably in markers on white paper
- Child's chair or small piece of furniture
- White latex paint—matte finish
- Scissors
- Flat brush
- Collage gel by Crafter's Pick
- Spray varnish, Crystal clear by Krylon

Clay Plates In a Row

Children are naturally drawn to the tactile feel of clay. It is irresistible to smash, smoosh, and squish the slippery mud. Clay, and the earthenware made from it, has been an essential means of carrying, serving, and storing everything from food to ashes. If you do not have a kiln, there is no need to avoid working in clay. There are many

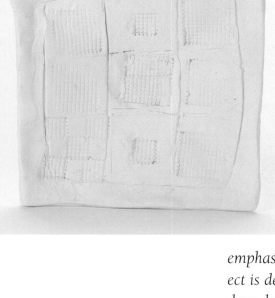

shops that offer ceramic studio time, and there are many types of clay available that do not require firing. The glazes available that color the pieces range from traditional underglaze to non-fire ceramic finish. Everyone should have the confidence to create at least one clay piece sometime in childhood. This project employs something I nicknamed a "formula." I find that with certain design structures, an appealing composition is built in and no matter what is done to embellish it, it is always a success. The clay is fashioned into little plates, suitable for framing (particularly in a shadow box).

This design structure is a sequence of the square, a square form, a square border, and a square frame, somewhere in the center of the work. This composition emphasizes objects by creating a "frame within a frame." The project is designed for children 4-5 years of age, and although the children do very little of the actual composition, they add the most creative part of the design. If the child is capable, you can direct the child to independently create the project. They discover that texture and shape can be produced by something as ordinary as a button.

Instructions

1. Prepare the clay into a slab so that it has no air bubbles. This is done by slamming it on a firm table and literally mashing the air out of the clay. Once it is prepared, roll or spread it into a slab on the craft foam.

2. Using the end tip of the plastic paintbrush as a tool, score through the clay and make three small plates, approximately 3" square. Store any remaining clay in an airtight bag for later use.

3. Using the end tip of the brush again, lightly etch a square around the border of each of the squares. You can also use the length of the brush handle and cross the lines; vary the style as desired.

4. Etch a tiny 1" square anywhere inside the plate. It can be off to a side, in a corner, or in the middle. Create the square in a different place in each of the plates.

5. Thread the wire through the buttons.

6. Using a scrap piece of clay, show the child how to press the button into the clay to get an impression. Pull the button free with the wire. Illustrate how to use the edge of the button to create texture by simply indenting the edge into the clay.

7. Allow the child to decorate the plates with the button impression or more "lines" with the end of a paintbrush.

8. Release the plates from the foam. Since the foam does not absorb or create a bond to the clay, this is very easy.

9. Allow the plates to dry. You can place it back on the foam, or a plastic craft needlework canvas.

10. Fire the plates.

11. Glaze or paint the plates if desired. You can even paint the plate with two colors by painting a "top" coat and removing the "high spots." Fire again if required.

12. Mount in a shadow box with wire wrapping or use a ceramic glue.

Materials

- Earth clay (dries to white or light gray clay before firing)*
- 8" x 11" sheet of craft foam
- Plastic paintbrush (we will use the handle)
- Two buttons with holes
- Two 8" pieces of thin wire (thin enough to go through the button-holes)
- Thin gauge wire in earth tones
- Duncan ceramic glaze

Note: This project can also be done with polymer clay.

Paper Balloon Bowl

Kids love balloons. This is one of those projects that, upon looking at the beautiful bowls, you appreciate not only the art but also the reminiscence of how fun balloons are—and what a part of childhood they are.

The balloon is actually used as a prop to form a structure for papier-mâché or air-dry clay. There are many types of papier-mâché and they all work. The main difference is they dry at different rates and they have a different texture to work with. The cost varies slightly but they are all very inexpensive materials. There are so many beautiful papers on the market that the bowls can be a beautiful mixture of children's writing and handmade papers. It is great for newsprint art. It is also a good way to salvage bits and pieces of art that really aren't in any composition, but perhaps the colors are wonderful.

The inside of the bowls are lined with gold leaf. This is a lot of fun to turn children loose with, because they can't harm anything (or be harmed by anything), and the gold leaf is mysterious to them.

Photo by Jay Jones. Robbie. M.

Instructions	Materials

Instructions

1. Blow up the balloons—but not too full. The balloon will need some give since some of the paper mixtures are heavy.

2. Cover the balloon with papier-mâché or paper clay. You can place it in a bowl or container to dry with the paper side up.

For traditional papier-mâché:

3. Make a paste mixture of diluted white glue or wallpaper paste. Cut strips of newsprint, dip in the paste and layer on the balloon. The layers are built up as each dries. This can take a number of sessions and kids may get impatient. But it is a good project to develop endurance and see results over a period of time.

For air-dry clay:

4. Roll a sheet of air-dry clay and lay it over the wide part of the balloon. Cut the folds with a scissors and overlap the clay. Smooth and pinch it together to connect the seams. Use water to smooth the clay. Air-dry clay is very smooth and dries very white. Note: Air-dry clay is very sensitive to the atmosphere. If the area is humid, the clay will stay moist longer. If the air is dry, it will require a mist of water to keep it workable. Keep unused portions of the clay under a damp towel when working. Store unused portions in an airtight container with a damp sponge. Prolonged storage may cause the clay to grow moldy.

5. All the clays take a while, even as long as a few days to dry. This requires some patience, but it is nice to see a "work in progress."

6. When the bowls are dry, pop the balloon.

7. Cover the outside with a collage of memorabilia. Tear sections of printing, art, and handmade papers. Use Crafter's Pick tacky glue or Perfect Paper Adhesive to paste the papers to the bowl. If a final coat is desired, you can coat with Perfect Paper Adhesive, or Craft Shield acrylic spray.

8. Add a coat of pigment powders, especially interference powders, to give a reflective, iridescent look to the finish.

9. Coat the inside with gold leaf adhesive and allow the bowl to dry. It only takes a few minutes.

10. Cover the inside with sheets of gold leaf. The leaf will adhere to the adhesive. Varnish the leaf for protection.

Materials

- Small balloons
- Delight air-dry clay or Creative paper clay
- Pearlex pigment powder, brush
- Handmade papers
- Child art on newsprint
- Gold leaf adhesive, varnish
- Gold composition leaf
- Tacky glue - Crafter's Pick or Perfect Paper Adhesive

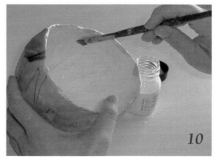

Tissue Plate

Photo by Elizabeth Heffernan. Khira and Rosio.

Art to me is not just one drawing, but an accumulation of a number of experiences. It is knowing how to sort and reassemble this information into a new structure that constantly creates new art. This is an interesting project that will mix and match the art of the child and the creativity of the adult. The art belongs to my niece, 2000 miles away. I rarely see her, but, just by doing this project, I feel a deeper connection to her and wonder what she will think of this plate 20 years from now. The finished piece resembles exquisite, iridescent glass. It was a completely spontaneous project. I don't think I would ever have dreamed of achieving such a piece, but with the inspiration of Kelsey's drawing, layers of experiences brought the project to life.

Note: This was done with a traced drawing but you could also accomplish it with a direct drawing or a stamped design. The "texture rubbing" can also be done by the child. This is a good way to teach children about texture and patterns. Try using lace or grainy sandpaper to discover different textures. You can also use colored tissues for interesting effects.

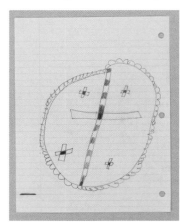

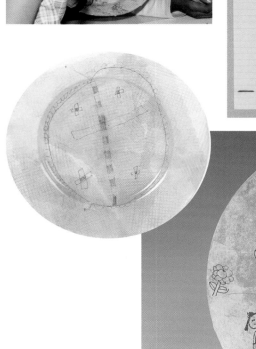

Instructions

1. Don't even bother to flatten crumpled tissue; the texture makes a great surface for coloring. Place the tissue on the plastic needlework canvas and use the side of the pastel sticks to rub the tissue. The grid of the canvas will show through. This is called a texture rubbing.

2. While coloring pastels, overlap the colors randomly. You will need approximately two square feet to cover a 10" plate.

3. Trace the drawing onto the colored tissue with the fine-point pen.

4. Cut the tissue into shapes using the special-edged scissors. These scissors work on a repeat pattern so you must begin the continuing cut aligned with the last cut. You can also tear the papers.

5. Clean the plate, and brush liquid laminate on the back of the plate.

6. Place the tissue drawing, ink and pastel (front) side, next to the wet laminate-coated plate.

7. Brush more laminate on the back of the tissue; spread the laminate carefully so the tissue doesn't rip.

8. Add layers of tissue and laminate until the whole plate is covered. Overlap layers of tissue. Allow the plate to dry.

9. When dry, trim the edge with an Excel craft blade. Use decoratively. It can be cleaned with a soft, damp brush.

Materials

- Child's abstract line drawings, abstract or garden theme
- Clear glass plate without obvious seams
- Liquid Laminate by Beacon
- Application brush
- Tissue paper
- Fiskars special-edged scissors (optional)
- Iridescent pastels from Sakura
- Micron Pigment fine-point pen 005 — Sakura
- Plastic needlework canvas — various grids
- Excel craft blade

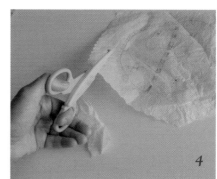

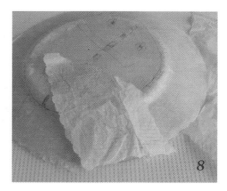

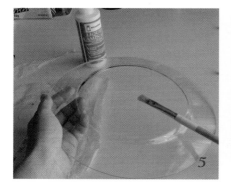

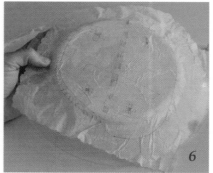

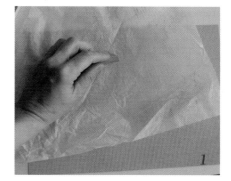

Pastel Felt Pillow

With today's products being so innovative, this is a perfect project for trying a few different techniques. This project introduces children to a medium other than paper. Pillows are always useful accessories, and with children's art they become quite colorful. The special-edged scissors create a festive finish of both the drawing and the pillow. I chose felt because it is soft. The picture is drawn with a heat-set pastel that can be cured in the oven or with an iron. Because the pastels are translucent pigment, the color will blend if it is overlapping. The beauty is that there is no mess at all. The pastel clings to the felt and once it is heat set, it is permanent. You can also use a fabric marker, but I felt the blending was softer with the pastels. The piece is attached to the pillow with fabric glue.

Photo by Jay Jones. McKenzie L.

Instructions	Materials

Instructions

1. Ask the child to draw anything she likes on the felt using the pastels. You may wish to set certain goals, such as "fill the whole page," or "fill the whole page with circles," or "fill the whole page with flowers." If you wish a certain color palette, choose that in advance and only give the child a few colors. If you are using heat set pastels, the chalk will sink into the fiber and remain intact. Set the pastels by placing the art in the oven on a piece of card stock paper and set the pastel for 10 minutes at 265° F. You can also use an iron. Place the art face down on an old sheet and set the iron to a low temperature. Iron gently on the back side of the work a few minutes until the color is set. Markers may slide on the top surface of the fiber. I actually did a test strip before I began.

2. Cut the edge of the art with Fiskars special-edged scissors to give it a playful, festive border.

3. Next, assemble the pillow jacket. Measure the size of the pillow. Use a cloth measuring tape to allow for the curve of the pillow.

4. Exceed the dimensions by 2" on each side.

5. Cut two squares (or pillow shape) of fleece to the dimensions determined by the size of the pillow. You will have one top and one bottom.

6. Prepare the bottom piece by placing the material fleece side down and spread glue on three edges.

7. Place the top piece as neatly on top of the bottom as possible and smooth the pieces together to seal the glue.

8. Spread glue on the back of the drawing and position the art in the center of the top fleece. Allow the glue to dry. Cut the glued border of the pillow with the decorative scissors.

9. Slip the pillow into the case.

10. Staple the open edge together at least one inch in from the edge of the border. Glue the border together as before. When it is dry cut with the scissors.

11. Remove the staples.

Materials

- 8" x 11" rectangle of lightly colored felt
- Duva ChromaCoal heat set pastels
  Alternatives:
    Fabric pens by Marvy
    Identipen by Sakura
    Pentel Dye sticks
- Fiskars special-edged scissors
- Fleece for pillowcase
- Muslin pillow core
- Cloth measuring tape
- Stitchless Fabric Glue
- Popsicle stick for spreading glue
  Alternative:
    Graphix Double stick adhesive
- Stapler
- Card stock paper (or old sheet for iron heat setting)
- Oven or iron for heat setting

Note: The pillow can also be sewn together.

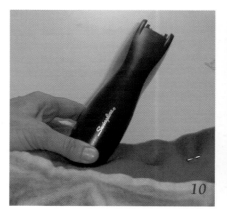

Poem Book

One day my son came home with the most beautiful poem about magical gifts that he had made into a card. It inspired the poem in the Dedication of this book. I am very grateful to the teacher, Audra Grandi, who presented this gift for children to make. It was in my son's best printing and ended with the words, "because you are my mom." The card was immediately endearing

and I wanted to keep it forever. But it was printed on lined, grade school newsprint and pasted to blue construction paper. I decided to transfer the poem to clay with a copier machine technique and make it permanent. I chose to frame it in an inset journal with a metal rubbing that I asked my son to participate in. This

journal ended up being the focus of many of my proposals throughout the year, but it always has remained this intensely personal memory of "you are my mom."

Materials

- A poem written in your child's printing—anything is okay
- Beige polymer clay
- A reversed copy of the poem (recommended Cannon copier) tone based
- A small journal (project shown has inset cover)
- Oven for baking clay
- Tracing paper and pencil, scissors
- Crafter's Pick Ultimate Tacky
- A rubber stamp, ink, stylus, and craft foam
- Art emboss foil, copper
- Burnt sienna acrylic paint
- Damp cloth
- Soft steel wool

Instructions

1. Plan the size you would like the poem to be and adjust it to your needs with a computer or copy machine.

2. Photocopy the poem on the reverse or "mirror" image setting. This is because when you transfer it to the clay, it will "mirror" again.

3. Condition and roll a thin sheet of polymer clay, approximately 1/16" thick, large enough to cover the size of your planned composition.

4. Place the photocopy face down on the clay and rub the backside of the paper so there are no air pockets that would prevent the toner from transferring.

5. Let the paper and clay sit for one hour. If the transfer has not released after that amount of time, you may need to bake it with the paper on and peel the paper after baking. You can soak and remove the paper if it does not release. The quantity of time needed for the transfer depends on the clay and the copier used.

6. Make a template for the size of the piece out of tracing paper. Position the tracing paper/template over the poem and cut the clay to the size of the template. I strategically placed my template so that the words "because you are my mom" would be showing.

7. Spread the area on the journal to be covered in clay with glue and let dry.

8. Place the clay on the glue. Note: If you have a pre-baked panel, you will glue the pieces together at one time as the final step of the project.

9. Cut a piece of the metal sheeting to fit the size of the stamp.

10. Freehand tracing with a stylus: the secret to this technique is to place the foil on a piece of smooth, dense, craft foam that will absorb the pressure of the stylus or ball pen.

11. Stamp the design directly on the foil.

12. Go over the inked lines with the stylus using firm pressure. If your child is doing this, you can explain that it is just tracing and that it may take a few times to practice and get a nice piece. The resulting effect is a little more like "dented" than embossed, but that's fine.

13. Cut a piece of cardboard and wrap the embossed metal around it, embossed side facing upward. Fold the sides in on the back. Coat the embossed square with a thin layer of burnt sienna acrylic paint. When the paint is dry, wipe the raised surface with a damp cloth. Lightly sand with steel wool to expose the copper and accentuate the relief.

14. Apply Crafter's Pick to the back of the metal and paper design. Place the metal piece on the clay, over the poem, and press gently into place.

15. Bake at 265° F. for 20 minutes or as the manufacturer directs. The book, which is paper, can also be placed in the oven, because paper will not burn at this temperature.

Note: There are several ways to do this project with different materials or techniques; for example, if you have a computer and a scanner, you could use T-shirt transfer paper to transfer the poem to the clay (set printer on mirror image). You could also choose to decoupage the poem directly. I recommend working with copies and keeping the original. Don't be limited by the instructions; your application is a personal choice.

7

10

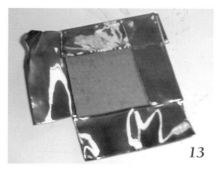

13

14

Shrink Heart Necklace

All kids love hearts and so do Moms. This is a necklace strand of hearts but it could also be made into an elastic bracelet. The colored wire adds a playful and festive complement to the delightful children's art. The children love to operate the tools, and the coiling gizmo makes winding wire fast and fun.

Photo by Jay Jones. Christine H.

Photo by Jay Jones. Tim M.

Instructions	Materials

Instructions

1. Sand one side of the shrink plastic with the manicure sponge to roughen the surface enough to accept color.

2. Punch or cut 12-24 hearts. Cut holes near the top of the heart with a paper punch. Even though the plastic is strong, it can be cut with most punches. If you are using a large heart punch, save the frame to make another project.

3. Give the hearts to the children to color and draw on. Since the available drawing area is small, the spatial relations in their drawings will be interesting.

4. Bake the shrink plastic at 275° F. for 5-6 minutes. Allow to cool and then sand the tips of the hearts just enough to remove the sharp points.

5. Cut 24 pieces of wire, 2" in length.

6. Attach the wire to the hearts. Hook the wire over and through as illustrated and wrap around the neck.

7. Coil the wire through the heart and around a straw to make a carrier for the heart. You want the heart to be able to dangle.

8. Coil sections of different colored wire and clip them into various lengths.

9. String the hearts and the coiled sections on a long piece of elastic to make a necklace.

10. Make a bracelet in the same manner, using a smaller version.

Variation:

Use shapes other than hearts, such as shells or stars. Just be sure to round off any sharp corners before baking, and sand points after baking to avoid snags and scratches.

Materials

- Polyshrink clear shrink plastic
- Manicure sanding sponge
- Colored pencils or markers
- Large heart punch cutter, McGill
- Hole punch
- Elastic
- Coiling gizmo or wooden skewer
- Telephone wire or 22- to 24-gauge poly-coated wire
- Wire flush cutters

Warning: Do not use crayons or oil pastels.

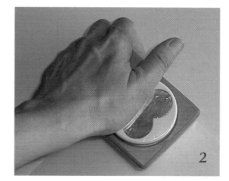

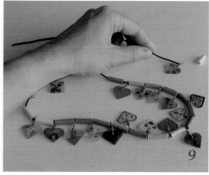

Buggy Frame

This project is great when you lead the child. They will respond to your direction but soon branch off into their own design. At first, the form of the body and eyes may be misshapen and enlarged. It is a good way to illustrate the subtle difference in proportions, and also refinement in size. For the most part kids don't care about these things. But if you illustrate it, they are interested in making their work really nice and they will follow your lead.

You may also notice that some children want to make as many as possible. They go for quantity. Others want to make one really special piece. It is recommended that each child get to do at least two bugs because one is just enough to practice.

Another tip to the appeal in this project is the color. Use muted colors to give the work a sophisticated look that can go in any décor. Kids can still have fun with the range of choices you present. The beautiful, soft colors are what make the bugs really unusual. The wire is also available in muted colors, although they are bright from the plastic coating. This coating helps them to stick to the polymer clay.

Instructions

1. Mix colors of clay by adding small bits of the primary colors to the gray. You will be surprised at the results, as the gray mutes the color. If you want deeper color, don't use as much gray.

2. Begin to roll balls and snakes and tiny bits into dots. You have to teach the child how to roll a ball and how to smooth the outside. The choices are still theirs, but they can be aware of the difference in a smooth piece as opposed to a distorted piece.

3. Shape the balls into a body by pinching and squeezing. Use the table to flatten the bottom. The bottom should be flat for mounting.

4. Build the body parts, head and eyes. If you mount the eyes and use tiny dots to accentuate the eyeballs, the bug will be more interesting. These are concepts that you show the child and they grasp. Once they have understood it, they will continue to make smaller parts, like teeth and ears.

5. Choose several colors of wire that are complementary to the project. The wire should highlight the colors in the body. Cut short lengths of wire, about 2", and twist and curl the wire by wrapping it around a pencil, straw, or another piece of wire.

6. Instruct the child to poke the wire pieces into the clay. This won't take much instruction—they tend to do this very well—but you may need to make a few suggestions to add decorative wiggles in strategic places.

7. Make more than one bug, because the first one is for learning, the second one is for expression.

8. Bake the pieces at 265° F. for 20 minutes.

9. When the piece has cooled, mount it to a picture frame, or a shadow box. Use Superglue, two-part epoxy, or Crafter's Pick to hold the bug in place in a shadow box frame.

Note: If the "hole" for the wires get too big you can add more clay in dots, or glue it in afterwards with superglue.

Materials

- Fimo soft metallic gray, small bits of red, blue, green
- Toner Fun Wire in "Icy colors"— these are muted "jelly"-like colors
- Flush cutters, round nose pliers (for wire)
- Superglue or Crafter's Pick
- Picture frame

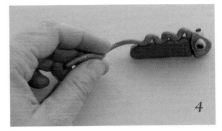

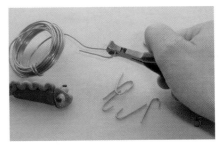

Directions for Covering Frame with Polymer Clay

1. Prepare wood or paper frame by coating it with a thin layer of Crafter's Pick glue. Allow it to dry.

2. Roll several thin sheets of polymer clay, enough to cover the frame. A pasta machine is very helpful to get the clay conditioned and evened into sheets.

3. Place the sheets on the frame. You will have to cover the frame in sections. Smooth the seams where the clay is sectioned. When the frame is covered, bake it at 265° F. for 20 minutes. Attach the bugs in the corners with Crafter's Pick Ultimate tacky and glue on strips of verse as desired:

I am a _____ critter. I have come to say _____.
You are_____!

Special note about papers and inks:

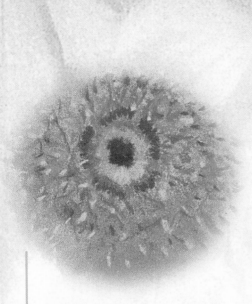

Papers

There is a great deal of variety in paper types.

—"Whiteness" or "brightness" in paper is rated on a 100-point scale. You can find good reams of white paper in office supply stores.

—"Poundage" refers to how heavy the paper is. Card stock paper is usually 40 lbs. to 130 lbs.

—"Tooth" means the texture or surface of the paper, whether it is smooth or rough.

—"Porous" is how absorbent the paper is. If the paper is glossy, it may not absorb the ink, and instead of being crisp, it will smear. You must choose the right ink with the right paper.

Inks

Inks are partners to paper, and now inks are being made that can also print on fabric.

—Dye ink will stain or dye the surface. Dye ink will work very well on absorbent paper and will stain most smooth paper surfaces as well.

—Pigment ink can also be used on porous surfaces, but pigment ink will slide off of glossy surfaces. To make the ink permanent you must cure the ink with heat. Use a heat gun made for rubber-stamping and embossing pigment inks. The gun is hotter than a hair dryer and will set the ink. This is also used to set ink on fabric. Hold the gun far enough away from the fabric to prevent scorching and heat for a few minutes. Be careful not to direct the heat toward your fingers, as the gun is hot enough to burn.

—Embossing powders are granulated powders that will melt when heated, and will then adhere to the surface. They are held in place by embossing ink or pigment ink. They need to be heat-set with a heat gun. To use embossing powders, first ink the image with pigment ink or embossing ink. Stamp the image to the paper. Sprinkle embossing powder over the entire inked surface. It will cling only where there is ink. Be careful not to smear it. Use a heat gun to set the powder. You will see the powder turn glossy and dark as the heat melts it.

Cut Shapes Cards

It is always a special treat for young children to work with interesting materials. Not only does it build dexterity, and fine motor skills, but also it keeps them occupied. The following cards were really impressive and fun to make as well as give. The elegance of the nested papers goes beyond the typical folded paper to make a card that's special.

Directions:

1. In advance cut and fold the cards and the printed verse that will nest inside.

2. Allow the children to cut strips and shapes of the holographic papers. Suggest cutting triangles or other odd shapes as well.

3. Show them how to peel the release paper from the cut out pieces.

4. Allow the child to adhere the shapes to the front of the folded card.

5. Nest the verse inside the folded card.

6. Punch two holes 1/2" from the seam, each hole one inch from the top and bottom edge.

7. Fold the front panel and the first page back over the holes, 1" from the seam and burnish with a bone folder to burnish the crease.

8. Allow the child to wrap wire through the holes and finish with a spiral to hole the pages in the card.

9. Ask the child to decorate the blank pages with drawings.

Materials

- Card stock paper (cut in half and folded to make a card)
- Printed verse, approximately 3" x 4" on white card stock paper. The verse was printed in the right hand "quarters" of the paper with enough room to cut and fold the card
- Fiskars Kidzors special-edged scissors
- Reynolds metallic and holographic paper—adhesive backed
- Paper punch
- Poly-coated wire, 4" lengths

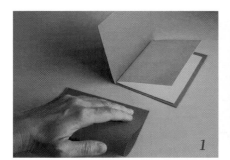

Photo by Barbara McGuire.

Mini Wire Wonders

There's a little wire sculpture on my desk that makes me smile. It could be a paperweight, it could even be drilled to be a pencil holder (like in the olden days) — but nonetheless it bears the mark of a child, and that makes it delightful. This is a project you do with a child and they make "theirs" along side of "yours."

Photo by Barbara McGuire.

Directions

1. Make some colorful polymer clay beads in advance, various shapes and sizes. Use a piece of 18 gauge wire to poke the bead holes to make sure the beads will fit on the wire. Dust the beads with iridescent powder if desired. Bake as directed by the manufacturer.

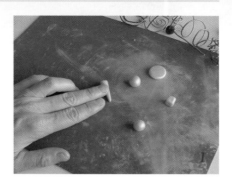

2. Condition and roll the scrap polymer clay into a mound.

3. The large 18-gauge wire will serve as the sculpture wire and the smaller wire will be used for wrapping.

4. Cut several lengths of 18-gauge wire.

5. Wrap the smaller wire around the larger wire, or wrap it around a straw or pencil.

6. Thread beads through the wire.

7. Bend the wire so that the beads hold in place.

8. Wrap wire around the beads, as in a "cage."

9. Poke the wire into the clay mound deep enough so that it sticks.

10. Put on the dust mask and use a cotton swab to apply Pearlex powder to the clay.

11. If you want to make a pencil holder, poke a pencil deep into the clay in two or three spots.

12. Bake the sculpture as the manufacturer directs. (The wire will withstand low oven temperatures.

13. When the piece is cool wipe the excess powder from the base of the pencil holder.

Materials

- Plastic coated wire, assorted colors, 24 gauge
- Plastic coated wire (Fun Wire) 18 gauge – any color
- Wire flush cutters
- Optional – coiling gizmo, or pencils and straws to serve as a mandrel
- Pre-made Colorful clay beads, large center holes (large enough to fit wire through)
- Scrap (discarded or unsightly mixed colors) Polymer clay or any color Sculpey (Polyform)
- Pearlex iridescent powder (non toxic powder but dust mask is advised)
- Cotton swab
- Dust mask

Note: if you do not have iridescent powder, you can wrap the scrap clay with a thin layer of beautiful metallic clay, to hide the scrap and still have a nice surface.

Miniature Art

Alexis F., age 4.

This project capitalizes on the charm of tiny images. The material is a plastic that shrinks to approximately one-half its original size, and firms into a solid strength suitable for making jewelry. You can use many types of color to decorate the surface, but it must be able to withstand curing temperatures of at least 350° F. The most familiar colorants are colored pencils and markers. The delightful drawings were first scanned to save the original art and then reduced to a size that, when shrunk again, would produce a finished piece, 1-1/2" square. The plastic can be baked again with no additional shrinkage, and is shown set in a polymer clay brooch.

Instructions

1. Scale the original art with a computer or a copier machine. The shrink plastic will reduce 50 percent. Prepare the Polyshrink by sanding the surface with a fine or medium manicure sponge. Wipe clean with a dry cloth but DO NOT WET. The sanding will give the plastic a "tooth" to grab the pigment of the colorant. Note: Lower grades of colored pencils require a coarser tooth.

2. Trace and color the drawing with the colored pencils or markers. Use a light box to trace on the white shrink plastic.

3. Once the art is completely colored, cut the edges to the desired shape. Use special edged scissors by Fiskars to create interesting borders.

4. Shrink the art in an oven for 5-6 minutes.

5. Prepare the polymer backing while the art is cooling.

6. Knead the clay until it is malleable and roll each color into a flat sheet about 3/16" thick. The sheet should be large enough to hold the design including a border or edge.

7. When the miniature art is cool, place it on the polymer clay and press firmly.

8. Carefully hold the piece and cut the edges with the special-edged scissors.

9. Bake on card stock paper at 265° F. for 20 minutes.

10. When the piece is cool, attach the pin back to the backside of the work with Superglue.

Tip: Polyshrink comes in clear, white and black. You can color both sides for a layered, translucent effect. Use the clear Polyshrink and sand one side. Draw and color on that side and when the piece shrinks, the color will show through the shiny side. Use gel pens on the black shrink plastic.

Materials

- Polyshrink with white background (Lucky Squirrel)
- Manicure sponge for sanding
- Child's drawing scaled to size
- Fiskars or special-edged scissors
- Prisma colored pencils or Sakura Identipens
- Markers
- Premo Black and Red polymer clay
- Polymer clay blade
- Roller (or cylindrical clear drinking glass)
- Pin back
- Superglue

Warning: Do not use oil pastels, or crayons, or any oil-based product. DO NOT WET.

Bibliography

Fineberg, Jonathan. *The Innocent Eye:Children's Art and the Modern Artist.* Princeton: Princeton University Press. 1997.

Frohardt, Darice Clark. *Teaching Art with Books Kids Love.* Golden, CO: Fulcrum Publishing. 1999.

Gardner, Howard. *The Arts and Human Development.* New York: Basic Books, Harper Collins Publishers, Inc. 1994.

-*Art Education and Human Development.* Los Angeles, CA: The J. Paul Getty Trust. The Getty Education Institute for the Arts. 1990.

-*Art, Mind, and Brain: A Cognitive Approach to Creativity.* New York: Basic Books, Harper Collins Publishers, Inc. 1982.

-*Artful Scribbles: The Significance of Children's Drawings.* New York: Basic Books, Perceus Books, L.L.C. 1980.

Carmozin-Helfman, Harry. *Making Pictures Without Paint.* New York: William Morrow & Co, Inc. 1973.

Kellogg, Rhoda, and Scott O'Dell. *The Psychology of Children's Art.* New York: CRM-Random House Publication. 1967.

Kellogg, Rhoda. *Analyzing Children's Art.* Mountain View, CA: Mayfield Publishing Co. 1969.

Kohl, MaryAnn F., and Jean Potter. *Global Art.* Beltsville, MD: Gryphon House. 1998.

Kohl, MaryAnn F. *Scribble Art: Independent Creative Art Experiences for Children.* Bellingham, WA: Bright Ring Publishing Inc. 1994.

Kohl, MaryAnn F. and Kim Solga. *Discovering Great Artists: Hands on Art for Children in the Styles of the Great Masters.* 1996 Bellingham, WA: Bright Ring Publishing Inc. 1996

Sark. *A Creative Companion: How to Free Your Creative Spirit.* Berkeley, CA: Celestial Arts. 1989.

Randall, Arne W., and Ruth Elise Halvorsen. *Painting in the Classroom: A Key to Child Growth.* Palo Alto, CA: Fearon Publishers, 1962.

Steward, Jan and Corita Kent. *Learning by Heart: Teachings to Free the Creative Spirit.* New York: Bantam Books. 1992.

Schirrmacher, Robert. *Art and Creative Development for Young Children.* Albany, NY: Delmar Publishers (International Thomson Publishing Co.) 1998.

Thomas, Jennie. *Helping Children Draw.* Dansville, NY: F. A. Owen Publishing Co. 1964

Footnote:
[1] Rhoda Kellogg with Scott O'Dell, *The Psychology of Children's Art*, CRM-Inc., 1967.

Resources

The following companies have contributed materials and efforts to the success of this book. It is to their credit that our children have quality products and services available. I wish to acknowledge and thank each one.

Jerri Stanard K-12 Gallery for Young People
Dayton, OH
(937) 461-5149
www.k12gallery.org

Mocha Museum of Children's Art
Oakland, CA
(510) 465-8770
www.mocha.org

Bay Area Discovery Museum
Sausalito, CA
(415) 289-7264
www.badm.org

San Francisco Children's Art Center
San Francisco, CA
(415) 771-0292

Colorific Children's Art Materials
Sanford Corporation, the world's largest writing
    instrument company.
Bellwood, IL
(800) 438-3703
www.sanfordcorp.com

Color & Co. Children's Art Materials
ColArt Americas, Inc.
Piscataway, NJ
(800) 445-4278
www.windsernewton.com

Creative PaperClay Co
Camarillo, CA
(800) 899-5952
www.paperclay.com

Dick Blick Art Materials
Galesburg, IL
(800) 447-8192
www.dickblick.com

Nasco Arts & Crafts
Modesto, CA
(800) 558-9595

Art & Creative Materials Institute
Hanson, MA
(781) 293-4100
www.acmi.net

International Child Art Foundation
Washington D.C. 20036
(202) 530-1000
www.icaf.org

Child Art Magazine (ICAF)
Washington D.C. 20033
childart@icaf.org

School Arts Magazine
Worcester, MA
(800) 533-2847

Inside Out
www.sfinsideout.org

Sakura
(Cray-Pas, Gelly Roll pens, Wonderful,
    Colorful World Contest)
Hayward, CA
(800) 776-6257
www.gellyroll.com

Duncan Enterprises
Ceramics and paints
Fresno, CA
www.duncanceramics.com

Fiskars Scissors
Wausau, WI
(715) 842-2091
www.fiskars.com

Reynolds Creative Essentials
Richmond, VA
(804) 281-3195
www.reynoldskitchens.com

Crafter's Pick API
Glues and adhesives
Albany, CA
(800) 776-7616
www.crafterspick.com

Perfect Paper Adhesive™
US ArtQuest
Grass Lake, MI
(517) 522-6225
www.usartquest.com

McGill, Inc.
Scissors and punches
Marengo, Il
(815) 458-7844
www.mcgillinc.com

PolyForm Products Co.
Sculpey™, Premo™
Elk Grove, IL
(847) 417-0020
www.sculpey.com

Beacon Adhesives
Mt. Vernon, NY
(800) 865-7238
www.beacon1.com

Barbara A. McGuire
Design Innovations
www.claystamp.com

Accent Import-Export, Inc.
FIMO
Pittsburg, CA 94565
www.fimozone.com

United Art & Education
Fort Wayne, IN
(800) 858-3247
www.unitednow.com

Artistic Wire
La Grange Park, IL
www.artisticwire.com

McCalister's Art Suppliers
Dayton, OH
(937) 278-0844

Kunin Felt
Hampton, NH
www.kuninfelt.com

Speedball
Statesville, NC
(800) 898-7224

DMD Industries
Paper Reflections®
Springdale, AZ
www.dmdind.com

Toner Plastics, Inc.
Agawam, MA
www.tonerplastics.com

PolyShrink, Lucky Squirrel
Albuquerque, NM
(505) 345-9455
www.luckeysquirrel.com

Council for Art Education
(781) 293-4100
www.acminet.org
(Youth Art Month)

Clay Factory
Escondido, CA
(877) Scul-pey
www.clayfactoryinc.com

Duva Fine Artist's Materials, Inc.
Albuquerque, NM
(877) 277-8374
www.lithocoal.com

Strathmore Artists Papers
Westfield, MA
(413) 572-9590

Artskills™
Art Makes You Smart™
www.artskill.com

ARTS ATTACK
(888) 760 ARTS

Safety and Toxicity

Every parent has questions about the toxicity of products their child may eventually use in connection with art projects. The following information is drawn from a booklet published by the ACMI. For additional information they can be reached at

1280 Main St., Second Floor, PO Box 479
Hanson, MA 12341
781-293-4100
www.acminet.org

"The Arts & Creative Materials Institute Inc., is a non-profit association of manufacturers of art, craft, and other creative materials. Since 1940, the ACMI has sponsored a certification program for children's art materials certifying that these products are nontoxic in the voluntary standards of quality and performance.

"The new AP (Approved Product), CP (Certified Product), AP (Approved Product) and H. L. Health Label (Non- Toxic) Seals identified art materials that are safe and that are certified in a toxicological evaluation by a medical expert to contain no materials in sufficient quantities to be toxic or injurious to humans including children, or to cause acute or chronic health problems. These products are certified by ACMI to be labeled in accordance with the chronic hazard labeling standard AST M.D. 4236 and the U.S. Labeling of Hazardous Art Materials Act (LHAMA). The new AP Seal is now being phased in my manufactures and will replace the former AP, CP and HL Seals within a ten-year period. Knowledge of materials and their proper use makes them safe. Be sure to read the label on all products you use so you will know that they have been evaluated and are nontoxic or need special handling to avoid possible health hazards from misuse. Follow all safe use instructions and purchase only products with the ACMI Non-Toxic Seals (CP, AP, and HL [Non-Toxic]) for young children, the physically or mentally handicapped, and any persons who cannot read or understand the safety labeling on product packages.

"The ACMI also gives recommendations for good habits concerning art materials:

Read the label and use products that are appropriate for the individual user.

Children in grades six and lower should use only nontoxic materials.

Do not use products that have passed their expiration date.

Do not eat or drink while using art and craft materials.

Washed up after use—clean yourself and your supplies.

Never use products for skin painting or food preparation unless indicated that the product is meant to be used in this way.

Do not transfer art materials to other containers. You will lose the valuable safety information that is on the product packages.

"Special note for a teacher or purchaser for schools: the law permits CPS to sue to prohibit the purchase of any art or craft material with the chronic hazard label warning for use in pre-kindergarten through sixth grade. These products can be purchased for using in grades seven through twelve. It may amount to professional malpractice for a teacher or school to ignore these requirements, aside from any civil or other liability concerns."

-ACMI

Encouraging creativity does not mean endangering a child; above all safety is an essential.

New Seal!